# PRAISE FOR *THE POWER OF GIVING AWAY POWER*

"Full of compelling stories and hard-won wisdom. Inspiring."

—Jon Favreau, cohost, *Pod Save America*

"Unexpected encounters! Barzun introduces you to people and ideas you never knew but should if you really care about leadership."

—Vint Cerf, internet pioneer

"A remarkable book about creating order without control and freedom without chaos, from an original and counterintuitive leader and thinker."

—Daniel H. Pink, author of *When, Drive,* and *To Sell Is Human*

"Matthew's leadership style has always been collaborative and celebratory of his teams, but in this wonderful book he shares the power of how lifting people up to lift up the entire organization."

—Nicole A. Avant, TV and film producer and former US Ambassador to the Commonwealth of the Bahamas

"An engaging, compelling, and welcome rebuttal to the distressingly widespread win/lose theories of leadership."

—Drew Faust, Arthur Kingsley Porter University Professor and President Emerita, Harvard University

"Redistributing power, an anthem of our times, gets a new twist from a former US Ambassador who rejects exerting power over whomever and whatever we can. Barzun engagingly argues for abandoning hierarchy to empower 'constellations' of diverse workers and teammates seeking the freedom to 'stand out and fit in.'"

—Anita L. Allen, JD, PhD, Henry R. Silverman Professor of Law and Professor of Philosophy, University of Pennsylvania

"The book is illuminating. It challenges you to take a hard look at your own leadership style . . . it's that good."

—Stacey Wade, CEO and executive creative director of Nimbus

"A riveting and unforgettable journey through the wisdom of largely-forgotten visionaries with profound potential to reshape modern leadership for the better."

—Jeffrey Rosen, president and CEO of the National Constitution Center

OPTIMISM
PRESS

# THE
# POWER OF
# GIVING AWAY
# POWER

# THE
# POWER OF
# GIVING AWAY
# POWER

*How the Best Leaders
Learn to Let Go*

## MATTHEW BARZUN

OPTIMISM PRESS

OPTIMISM
PRESS

Optimism Press
An imprint of Penguin Random House LLC
penguinrandomhouse.com

Most Optimism Press books are available at a discount when purchased in
quantity for sales promotions or corporate use. Special editions, which include
personalized covers, excerpts, and corporate imprints, can be created when
purchased in large quantities. For more information, please call (212) 572-2232 or
email specialmarkets@penguinrandomhouse.com. Your local bookstore can
also assist with discounted bulk purchases using the Penguin Random House
corporate Business-to-Business program. For assistance in locating a
participating retailer, email B2B@penguinrandomhouse.com.

Image on page 72 from *The 7 Habits of Highly Effective People* by
Stephen R. Covey. Used with permission.

Image on page 73 Copyright © 2001 by Jim Collins. Reprinted by
permission of Curtis Brown, Ltd. All rights reserved.

Image on page 131 by PIXbank CZ / Shutterstock

Image on page 182 by ESB Professional / Shutterstock

Library of Congress Cataloging-in-Publication Data

Names: Barzun, Matthew Winthrop, 1970– author.
Title: The power of giving away power / Matthew Barzun.
Description: New York : Optimism Press, [2021] |
Includes bibliographical references. |
Identifiers: LCCN 2020045752 (print) | LCCN 2020045753 (ebook) |
ISBN 9780525541042 (hardcover) | ISBN 9780525541059 (ebook)
Subjects: LCSH: Power (Social sciences) | Leadership. | Organizational behavior.
Classification: LCC HM1256 .B37 2021 (print) |
LCC HM1256 (ebook) | DDC 303.3—dc23
LC record available at https://lccn.loc.gov/2020045752
LC ebook record available at https://lccn.loc.gov/2020045753

Printed in the United States of America
1st Printing

BOOK DESIGN BY ELLEN CIPRIANO

*For B.B.B.*

Though analogy is often misleading,
it is the least misleading thing we have.

—SAMUEL BUTLER

# CONTENTS

# A LETTER FROM SIMON SINEK

*The vision is clear: to build a world in which the vast majority of people wake up every single morning inspired, feel safe wherever they are, and end the day fulfilled by the work that they do. The only way to build this world is if we work together. But there's a problem. . . .*

*Over the past few decades, our society has overindexed on rugged individualism. Images of the lone cowboy in a Marlboro commercial became an ideal to strive for. We emulated the big personality leaders who presented an image of the "strong man," the genius in the room. As the "high-performing individual" became the standard, company structures transformed to feed the beast. They adapted their incentive and reward systems to recognize individual performance almost exclusively. Ethics, teamwork, and leadership qualities seemed to fall to the wayside when we evaluated people for promotion. Even our business schools became complicit. Over the years, they adapted their curricula to serve the market rather than teach leadership as it should be taught. However, if it's long-term results, stability, or innovation we're hoping to achieve, this model of leadership simply doesn't work. The unfortunate irony is, the opposite model doesn't work either. Consensus-building, leaderless* organizations, tribal leadership, even the much touted "bottom-up" approach, all suffer complications in their own ways. The good news is, there is another option. This is where The Power of Giving Away Power *comes in.*

Matthew Barzun has spent decades figuring out where big ideas come from. Once he learned the concept of giving away power, he applied it to his own career. And it worked. Matthew's ideas played a significant role in helping CNET grow into a powerhouse media platform. Challenging the traditional way money was raised for political campaigns, Matthew pioneered a small-dollar/big-event fundraising platform that helped Senator Barack Obama significantly outpace Hillary Clinton's efforts with $5 and $10 donations. And as US Ambassador to the UK, Matthew practiced giving away power in a way the ambassadors just didn't do. The ideas that were generated as a result were astounding.

I had the opportunity to meet Matthew during the time he was the ambassador to Britain. I was astonished by his thinking. Whenever we would have occasion to talk, I would scramble to find a pen and paper so I could take notes on everything he said. This was why I asked Matthew to write a book for Optimism Press. The way he helps us better understand how the world works—how power works—can help move us closer to that vision—a world in which we feel inspired, safe, and fulfilled in our lives and our careers.

Give power and inspire on!
Simon Sinek

# INTRODUCTION

PRETENDING IS EXHAUSTING.

So it's surprising how many of us get up every day and do exactly that under the banner of leadership. Pretending that we know the precise destination, what steps in what order are required to get there, and how any unexpected obstacles can be cleared away as we drive toward an inevitably successful outcome. All the while projecting supreme confidence.

Around the year 2000, organizations of all kinds, from Rhode Island's historical society to the multinational conglomerate Siemens, churned out strategic planning reports for the decades ahead called "Vision 2020." The number proved an irresistible temptation to pretend we could see with perfect 20/20 vision into the future for our companies, communities, and countries. The glossy reports spelled out confidently what could be expected in 2020 and what to do to seize the coming opportunities. In 2018, with just two years to go, Harvard Business School published a guide asking "Is Your 'Vision 2020' Leadership Development Strategy on the Path to Success?" Then that year arrived with a vengeance as if to say, "Oh, yeah?"

In our hearts, we know how scarce certainty is. Even the ultimate leadership guru Peter Drucker, who first found fame advocating "management by objective," admitted that leaders know their true objective only 10 percent of the time at best. Still we hold on tightly to the theater of pretending and predicting. Why?

We do it because there is something we dislike even more than the exhaustion of pretending. Much more. We hate the anxiety of uncertainty. Pretending is the price we pay to remove it.

So we comfort ourselves with orderly org charts, working backward from a preset destination, factoring out what we can't measure, tasking team members using "key performance indicators"—monitoring it all with "dashboards," turning and tuning the dials as if running a machine. It is our way of self-soothing by exerting control and power over whatever and whomever we can.

We think we must hoard power before someone else takes it and that we must lord it over others. We've not only come to value the consolidation and preservation of power as the best kind of leadership; we've come to believe it's the only kind—that it *is* leadership.

How crazy.

All we have to do is look around to see that there are other kinds of leaders who have adopted a very different mindset about uncertainty. They don't try to ignore it, avoid it, or factor it out. They factor it in—radically. They do this not by hoarding and lording power, but by doing the opposite—by giving it away. In this way, they turn the anxiety of uncertainty into the energy that drives diverse groups of people to build unbelievably big things together.

In my twenty-five years of working across three different fields—dot-com startups, President Obama's campaigns, and international diplomacy—I've been a witness to great leaders who hold this mindset. They share a particular way of seeing, thinking, feeling, and behaving with the people around them. I have tried to practice this mindset—one that we are all capable of, and one that I am certain the world needs more of these days.

I saw this mindset at work up close in 2008. Barack Obama's campaign against Hillary Clinton for the Democratic Party's presidential nomination had reached a critical juncture. Obama won the first contest in Iowa in an upset, but lost the next one in New Hampshire. Pundits pounced. Barack and Michelle had camped out in Iowa for nearly a year and had deployed a huge chunk of their campaign staff there. Anyone can pull an upset in one state with a lot of focus and a little luck, but now the Clinton "machine" would surely kick into gear and normal political logic would take over.

In the course of nearly a decade, the Clinton team had locked up the key endorsements in each state, and now each of these state power brokers would, in turn, release their loyal legions of get-out-the-vote foot soldiers. How could the Obama campaign possibly match the proven math of that political pyramid?

Two young Obama staffers pitched a radical solution to the campaign leadership in Chicago that went against decades of modern campaign orthodoxy. They had been sent to states with almost no paid staff and had been noticing the same thing. Delegating work and responsibilities to unknown, unpaid, untrained volunteers was not generating the normal headaches. In fact, just the opposite: giving away work and responsibility led to more volunteers showing up and asking for more work and responsibility. It kept growing. What if we treated these volunteers more like paid staff?

But here was the most radical part: What if we even gave them access to the "voter file"? This is a campaign's preciously guarded data bank of possible voters, where they live, and how likely they are to vote for you.

The campaign leadership said no. There would be spies from rival campaigns. The state power brokers working on behalf of the Clinton campaign would certainly scoop up the data, essentially stealing our playbook. The staffers persisted. They admitted that their plan couldn't prevent that but made the case that a growing universe of committed and empowered people would be worth a lot more than any potential downside from data stealing. If they didn't open up the campaign, they would definitely have to turn people away. There was simply no other way of unleashing the energy and letting the campaign grow.

The campaign leaders had seen these young staffers work miracles already. They decided to place their faith in them and their way of thinking. "Okay, go for it." And they were glad they did, because it worked to win the party nomination. But the true test would be whether it worked on Election Day in November against the strength of a unified national party that had won the last two elections.

When that day came, the Obama campaign unleashed every volunteer to help get out the vote. There's a famous metric in field organizing called the *flake rate*, which refers to the percentage of pre-committed volunteers who flake out and don't show up to do the work they promised. A really bad flake rate is 80 percent, where eight in ten don't show up because they feel either all is lost or else it's in the bag. A really good flake rate could be as low as 30 percent. As a rule of thumb, you plan on 50 percent.

On election night, as we celebrated President Obama's historic win in Chicago, I was eager to know what our flake rate had turned out to be and asked one of the field team leaders. She had just gotten the data from her colleague in Virginia, one of the important swing states Obama won that night. "There wasn't one . . . or I guess you could say it was negative . . . negative fifty percent," she reported. Wait, what? She explained that for every ten people who committed to volunteering, fifteen people showed up. They did the opposite of flaking out. They showed up and brought new people in. They multiplied. With this different mindset, the campaign reached new mathematical territory. It made the flake rate obsolete.

This mindset of giving away power to create more is all too rare these days, but those young field organizers were not alone. There have always been people all around us who are making a huge difference by seeing things in a way the rest of us are missing.

With this different mindset, a middle manager at a midsize bank in a mid-tier city transformed the chaos of the early credit card business into the largest commercial enterprise the world has ever known.

With this different mindset, a commodities trader from Alabama found new energy in the apparent anarchy of the internet, beat out the richest company in the world, and in so doing spawned the largest human knowledge transfer engine the world has ever known.

And with this different mindset, a stockbroker made a house call to a doctor in Akron, Ohio, and they discovered a new method for mutual healing by placing uncertainty at the center of their conversations, creating the largest anti-addiction platform the world has ever known.

But these leaders didn't get there without a struggle. After experiencing the inevitable frustrations of forcing others to comply with their plan, their next instinct was to go it alone. We all do that. But eventually each leader made the same key insight. They discovered that independence is just another form of dependence—dependence on oneself, all alone. They discovered something more powerful beyond both dependence and independence.

With their help, we will too. And we will be guided by a woman who was one of the most influential leadership thinkers of her day. She is the intellectual interpreter and matron saint of this mindset. In fact, Drucker credits her with being his guru and the "brightest star" in the constellation of leaders, yet she was nearly erased from history.

To paraphrase another character you will meet later: I am in this book, but it's not about me. You are in this book, but it's not about you. It is about you and me and a third thing that is a character in itself—namely, "us, together." This book is about the power we can create by giving away power to this third character—which gives power back to us to be given away again. And again.

This book is a practical and sometimes personal history of an idea and a mindset. It chronicles my own growing awareness of an ineffable something that defines the leaders I most admire, and my attempt to give that a name and a shape. The journey takes us through history and across politics, industries, and national borders, mingling stories of near-forgotten gurus with stories from my life as an ambassador to Sweden and the UK and adviser to Obama's presidential campaigns. We will see not only how this mindset started some of the most consequential organizations and innovations the world has ever known; we will also see that it even started the greatest idea for a country the world has ever known. And that's where the story begins.

# THE
# POWER OF
# GIVING AWAY
# POWER

# 1

## THE LOST CONSTELLATION

ON JULY 4, 1776, the founders made not one but two declarations. They had spent so much time deliberating over independence that they hadn't done much thinking about the basics of putting themselves on the world map as a new country. They now realized it wasn't going to be enough to put this new experiment into words, even the immortal ones of the Declaration of Independence. To be taken seriously, they had to project a national image. And so, in a move familiar to startups everywhere, the second official declaration that day was: we need a logo.

Strictly speaking, it wasn't a "logo." They wanted an official "Great Seal" that would serve as a symbol of this new collection of now-independent colonies. It would be stamped in wax to adorn every foreign treaty and domestic proclamation.

It would replace the despised imprint of the crown of King George. It would project strength and unity to supporters and skeptics alike, whether in foreign capitals or at home in the thirteen colonies from New Hampshire to Georgia.

As we'll see, it took longer to design this logo than it did to win the war. And the story of the seal's coming to be is the story of overcoming a challenge that many of us are reckoning with now. Namely, how to have order—within our companies, committees, and communities—without hierarchy and strict authority, and how to have freedom without inefficiency or even chaos. The founders soon recognized that independence was the easy part and learned to give expression to something harder but much better: interdependence. And in so doing, they handed down a powerful symbol for the mindset needed to attain it. But let's not get too far ahead of ourselves.

In 1776, the Continental Congress was a slapdash collection of delegates from the colonies and there was no reliable process for getting things done. Instead, there was Charles Thomson, Secretary of Congress. Thomson's obscurity to us now is an odd blind spot of history (the publisher of his biography is called Forgotten Books) because he was among that generation's rising stars. Only two signatures appear on the first-printed Declaration of Independence: John Hancock's and Charles Thomson's.

As the Secretary of Congress, Thomson handed the logo assignment over to the A-team—Benjamin Franklin, Thomas Jefferson, and John Adams. These three giants of Enlightenment thinking had managed to capture their most sacred abstract principles in the concrete words of the Declaration, which are memorized in grade-school classes to this day. How did they fare at turning those words into a powerful image that would inspire a newborn nation?

Well . . .

When the team got together, Franklin went first. He advocated high drama—a biblical scene with Moses parting the waters as he escaped Pharaoh. Franklin's own notes capture his pitch to his colleagues: "Moses standing on the Shore, and extending his Hand over the Sea, thereby causing the same to overwhelm Pharaoh who is sitting in an open Chariot, a Crown on his Head and a Sword in his Hand. Rays from a Pillar of Fire in the Clouds reaching to Moses."

The seal, it should be noted, would be only two inches in diameter.

Jefferson went next. He suggested that the Great Seal ought to have two sides, like a coin. For the front, he stuck with biblical sources, but he thought it should depict the wandering children of Israel. For the back, perhaps revealing his own racialist flip side, Jefferson proposed Hengist and Horsa, obscure brothers of legend who established Anglo-Saxons in England.

Adams went classical. Inspired by a famous Italian painting, he proposed the towering figure of Hercules, who is forced to choose between the flowery road of ease and indulgence or the difficult uphill road of duty to others.

To sum up, the three choices for America's foremost symbol at this point were a drowning Egyptian, lost children backed by white nationalism, and an indecisive giant.

Like so many confused committees that have followed, they hired a consultant, who explained that there was a formula for making a seal. It had to have four elements: a shield, something to support that shield, a motto, and finally an element above the shield that serves as the essence of the overall thing, called a *crest*. They acquiesced to his formulaic suggestion for the design. It was boring, but safe. But they perked up when he suggested a potential motto: "E Pluribus Unum" (out of many, one). Enthusiastic nods to that.

The committee presented its compromise design to Congress. Despite the marquee names involved, Charles Thomson and his colleagues didn't like it. Not at all. Thomson didn't reject it outright but rather called for a vote so that it could, in the committee-speak of those times, "lie on the table." With a war on, the logo project stalled for the next three and a half years.

In 1780, Thomson handed the materials over to a second committee, which struggled for a few weeks and (yep) hired a consultant named Francis Hopkinson, a fellow signer of the Declaration of Independence who had arranged the 1777 version of the US flag. Hopkinson reworked the elements from the first committee, but his major innovation was the crest on the front of the seal, which became the prominent feature.

The design looked like this:

More expressive than the orderly rows of stars on his flag, the collection of stars not only represented the thirteen states but also their simultaneous independence and unity—their interdependence. Deliberately asymmetrical, the layout of stars expressed the essence of a new American way. Big states like Virginia and small ones like Rhode Island were each distinct but connected into a greater whole.

He called it a "radiant constellation."

The design was striking and beautiful, and it reflected the nation's originality and ambition. But it was also . . . different. It was not a lion or an eagle or a sword. It struck the delegates as a little too . . . bold. The wartime Continental Congress of 1780 wasn't ready for it. After all, Hopkinson may have signed the Declaration, but he was also an eccentric who had asked to be paid in wine. Thomson had the project "referred back to committee," where it languished again, but it stuck with him. His official minutes, preserved at the Library of Congress, show his doodles of versions of the seal in the margins.

Two years later, peace talks to end the American Revolution were underway in Paris, and now the pressure was ratcheting up. The founders would need the new Great Seal to stamp on the peace treaty. Thomson and the Continental Congress formed yet another committee to bring it home.

The third time was not the charm. Yet another consultant was brought in; he reverted to something traditional: an imperial eagle, a standard of old-world heraldry. They were more daring with the back, though, borrowing a symbol from the continental currency that had been devised by none other than Mr. Wine-for-Work himself, Francis Hopkinson. It was a thirteen-stepped pyramid signifying "Strength and Duration," unfinished at the top to symbolize the never-ending work of striving toward perfection. But the committee wanted to fill the empty space at the top with . . . something. Someone suggested a palm tree, but the committee preferred the all-seeing Eye of Providence in a triangle, a scrap from the first committee's efforts.

Even under the gun, Congress knew it wasn't right. With the clock running down, Thomson had to face the reality that this just wasn't working. He understood the opportunity and the stakes. The world was watching.

He was a true believer in freedom—and he was certain that people could be free together without a king or any rigid hierarchy. He had proved that belief earlier in his career when he was asked to work through disputes with Native Americans and earned honorary membership in the Delaware tribe and was given a name meaning "man who tells the truth." He proved that belief as a lifelong opponent of slavery, who would tell Jefferson it "must be wiped out" and that it was "a cancer we must get rid of."

He had seen that interdependence has its own character. This was his core insight that couldn't be outsourced to a consultant. His job now was to let each committee's voice be heard, so to speak, and to let them form something bigger than any one of them had done individually. He laid out all the designs, brought in a young local artist, and began mixing and matching elements with his own ideas.

In a nod to the first committee's wish for originality, he got rid of the human figures and moved the eagle down from the crest to be the lone supporter of the shield. He made it distinctively an American bald eagle and much more prominent in the design. From the A-team of wordsmiths, he took exactly zero of their design ideas but kept 100 percent of their words, choosing their motto, E Pluribus Unum—"out of many, one."

That left only one element to choose for the front—the crest, the essence of the whole thing.

He decided boldness had been earned. Congress was now ready for Hopkinson's wonderfully beautiful and different "radiant constellation." For Hopkinson, the constellation had partly symbolized the thirteen colonies. For Thomson, now it also partly symbolized the United States taking its rightful place among other nations for trade and treaties. For both, it was most importantly a symbol of the animating idea of this new country: independent bodies freely choosing to behave in concert to accomplish something bigger than each could alone. One could stand out on one's own—a star—but at the same time be part of a larger unit—a constellation. And the image was open-ended, offering room for more stars and, just as important, room for new and varying connections between them.

He thought the third committee's back of the seal (the pyramid and the all-seeing eye on top) was worth keeping, and it provided space for two more mottoes, Novus Ordo Seclorum (a new order of the ages) and Annuit Coeptis (providence has favored our undertakings). Even though the pyramid was a symbol of consolidated, concentrated power, the likes of which the founders were always suspicious, Thomson liked it for what it conveyed about "strength and duration." After all, the country might need that kind of top-down solidarity in certain times of crisis. It had its place—the back. Here is Thomson's sketch:

On June 20, 1782, after six years, the Congress approved the design of the Great Seal of the United States. Immediately and unanimously. They promptly cut the front of the seal into brass (but didn't bother doing the same for the back).

It hasn't changed all that much in 240 years.

In a letter to Ben Franklin around the same time, Thomson wrote that he had never worried about winning the war, but he was afraid victory "would come upon us before we were prepared to receive it, and before we had acquired national principles, habits and sentiments" necessary to act interdependently.

Victory hadn't come too early. Guided by the image of the constellation, the Congress collaboratively created and approved the Constitution, which enshrined its principles—states and citizens and federal government, neither strictly dependent on nor independent of one another, linked in a constellation of their own.

During the deliberations, the delegates created a rotating president of the Congress and chose for that position another seal. It had only one side. And only one image and one motto: the constellation and "out of many, one."

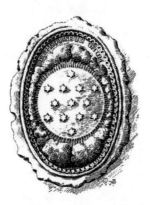

A bit hard to read from this sketch of the Seal of 1782,
but "E Pluribus Unum" is written at the top.

"The seventeenth of September, 1787," doesn't quite have the same ring to it as the Fourth of July, 1776, but that was the day they signed the final draft of the Constitution, and it's actually more sacred in many ways. Any band of revolutionaries can declare independence. Only one was able to invent a government and a legal system that realized the ideas represented by the constellation. It really ought to be remembered as America's Interdependence Day.

Thomson was the only person to serve continuously in all the iterations of the Continental Congress from 1774 all the way through the fifteen years until George Washington was elected president under the new Constitution. One biographer called Thomson our first and only prime minister. Congress asked him, as one of his last official acts, to get on his horse and tell Washington that he'd been elected the first president of the United States and to make it official by transferring to him the brass stamp for the Great Seal.

In one of his first acts as president, Washington commissioned and named five new Navy frigates that would serve as sailing advertisements for the new constitutional government. Would he harken back to biblical or classical themes? Would he name them after individual heroes or abstract principles? No. He named them after the new American creations: the USS *United States*, the USS *Constitution*, the USS *President*, the USS *Congress*, and . . . the USS *Constellation*.

## THE PATTERN HOLDS

The great chronicler of the American soul, the Frenchman Alexis de Tocqueville, saw our Constellation (let's give it a capital

*C* like Washington did) pattern of interdependence at every scale when he visited the US in 1825. He was amazed by how unlike a European country it was. Almost nothing was built out of stone or brick—the traditional symbols of stability, durability, and power. Citizens were so restless and their movements so fluid that they built things out of wood. He recognized that the magic of the country wasn't in material things at all but in things of the spirit—things that were hard to quantify but whose practical impact was powerful. The United States had energy.

Just as impressive as the sheer amount of energy was the ability to use it by coming together. Based on the country's shared "principles, habits and sentiments," as Thomson had called them, Constellations were formed to deal with matters that in another country would be dependent on government or royal attention, or would be left to people to deal with on their own. Tocqueville saw this pattern at every scale: "Americans of all ages, all conditions, all minds constantly unite. Not only do they have commercial and industrial associations in which all take part, but they also have a thousand other kinds: religious, moral, grave, futile, very general and very particular, immense and very small."

To be sure, he did not look past the hypocritical and evil un-Americanness of the US's southern plantations. "I am pained and astonished by the fact that the freest people in the world is, at the present time, almost the only one among civilized and Christian nations which yet maintains personal servitude." But he saw that in most of America, uncertainty about status and social order was made into a virtue. "They easily shake off the influence which the habits of other nations might exercise upon their minds. . . . America is a land of wonders, in which everything is in constant motion, and every movement seems an improvement."

By breaking down traditional power, America was building up tremendous energy. This Constellation pattern of principles, habits, and sentiments achieved something big through many actions that were quite small. Each person gave them life and meaning. And this pattern didn't just make democracy work. It made business and social and spiritual life flourish too.

## ENTER THE PYRAMID

However, while this energetic Constellation culture continued to permeate American life, a different structure began to take shape alongside it. As mass production turned craftspeople into laborers, a new kind of hierarchy emerged, mirroring the efficiency of the machine. This consolidated order generated great concentrated wealth up through the 1920s—until it didn't. That's when the whole system came crashing down with the Great Depression.

Remember that when the Great Seal was approved, they

immediately cast a metal version of the front, with the Constellation. But they didn't cast the back, the pyramid side—not once—until 150 years after its creation. And only because of a chance encounter between a man and a book.

It was 1934, deep inside the building that housed the Departments of State, War, and the Navy across the street from the White House, and deep into the Great Depression. President Franklin Roosevelt was implementing the New Deal to get the country going and growing again. Agriculture secretary Henry Wallace sat in the secretary of state's waiting room before a meeting. He noticed a book, *The History of the Seal of the United States*, which the State Department had commissioned in 1876 as part of the centennial celebrations.

Wallace flipped through it as he waited and was surprised to learn that the Great Seal had a back side. Who knew? Then he got excited because under the pyramid was the motto Novus Ordo Seclorum. He knew some Latin from grade school and thought the phrase could be interpreted with license as "a New Deal for the ages." He held on to the book to show FDR. The boss was going to love this!

And love it he did. This newly rediscovered back of the Great Seal fit FDR's needs perfectly. The pyramid represented strength, duration, and hierarchical effort. And it was unfinished, but nearly done. The second motto, in addition to the freshly interpreted "New Deal for the ages," the one above the all-seeing Eye of Providence, gave further encouragement: Annuit Coeptis, "God approves."

FDR was doing as much as he could as quickly as he could. The country's raw economic output had been nearly cut in half in one year from 1929 to 1930. Unemployment shot up nearly 1,000 percent. In his first inaugural address, Roosevelt asked for emergency powers "to wage a war against the emergency, as great as the power that would be given to me if we were in fact invaded by a foreign foe."

FDR decided to fight a mass national emergency with massive programs centralized in Washington. Fight pyramid with pyramid. And the president wanted to get the pyramid—this symbol of consolidated power—out there to the public. As luck would have it, the US Treasury was about to put out a new one-dollar bill. FDR suggested they re-introduce the Great Seal in its full two-sidedness after 150 years of dormancy as part of the new release.

The Treasury obliged, and for the first time since the seal's creation, both sides would be displayed. Now the United States would depict two sources of strength as equals—the Constellation representing the new energy of an interdependent nation and the pyramid representing a different kind of stability, under consolidated power, even if that meant dependence under authority.

The Treasury Department sent Roosevelt a mock-up for approval. Notice anything strange about it?

Look closely at FDR's handwritten approval above—he gives the green light to the new greenback but with one condition (shown here in his doodled triangle approximation): put the pyramid first. And so they did. And there it remains.

Final product, issued 1935

To be clear, there was no conscious decision to push the United States in a new, hierarchical direction under the banner of this monolithic symbol, but FDR's choice commemorated a very real change rapidly taking place in the American mindset.

The pyramid mindset not only pushed us through a prolonged recovery but was also enlisted again when the emergency of the Great Depression gave way to the emergency of World War II. The war provoked mass mobilization of manufacturing, higher taxes, even bigger national agencies, and a centralized draft.

America barely had time to celebrate when the Cold War took hold. Domestic political power consolidated under Washington, DC, as did Western military might. A superpower was born. Grand displays of power were the points on the Cold War's scoreboard. The Constellation mindset had at this point clearly yielded to a different perspective driven by consolidated power. Pyramid first indeed.

# THE PYRAMID VS. THE CONSTELLATION

The differences between the Pyramid (only fair to capitalize too) and the Constellation mindsets go far beyond organizational structure. They encompass different ways of relating to people and the world around us. And so when we reorganized ourselves, we changed ourselves too.

Here's how we think and see in our Pyramid mindset: We fit people into functions, at work and in general. ("Nice to meet you. What do you do?") We make detailed plans working backward from a set destination. ("Good idea, but let's stick to the plan.") We define tasks to lock in predictable output. ("I've set your key performance indicator to X so that the division goal can be 5X.") We try to eliminate uncertainty by fixing our attention on structure, efficiency, and predictability and the power derived from them. It is hierarchical by nature (in-out, up-down, up-or-out) and obscures our ability to see outside the sharp lines it imposes.

Thinking in Constellations is very different. In the Constellation mindset, we set ourselves in motion toward possibility, not toward a set destination, allowing for many branching paths. Possibility attracts the energy of like-minded individuals. Engagement is voluntary. Leadership flows as dictated by evolving needs. With vision and reciprocal commitment, power is given away, then grows, then more is given back.

Both offer freedom but of very different kinds.

The Pyramid mindset offers freedom *from*. Consolidated dependence under a hierarchy offers a certain kind of security from outside threats. Less obviously, the Pyramid mindset is also with us in our independence. We become our own self-contained mini-pyramids (like the little triangle above the big pyramid in the Great Seal)—free, we imagine, from everything.

The Constellation mindset, on the other hand, offers freedom *with*. Each of us freely acts in concert with others based on shared principles, habits, and sentiments. This offers choice and autonomy with a different kind of security and stability.

## THE WEB AND THE WALL

Our speed-walk through American history isn't over just yet. As the US settled into its Pyramid mode, things took a new course. Everything seemed to change again in 1989, the year the Berlin Wall came down and the World Wide Web went up. After decades of hot and cold national emergencies, a new era was clearly on the horizon, offering opportunities for greater peace, freedom, and prosperity. Could the United States return to its native Constellation or had the Pyramid become our default setting for making sense of ourselves and the world around us?

A few years after the wall fell, Robert Putnam wrote the essay "Bowling Alone: America's Declining Social Capital," which, with painstaking research, catalogued the deterioration of Charles Thomson's Constellation "principles, habits and sentiments." It seemed that maybe the Pyramid had completely stamped out the old way and would reign supreme forever. But a few years later, in 2000, when Putnam's book based on the essay was published, it was called *Bowling Alone: The Collapse and Revival of American Community*. It was the height of the dot-com boom, and internet-enabled technology like the World

Wide Web, email, and hosts of new services suggested that maybe there was hope for the Constellation after all.

Along the way, we've all gotten savvier about the limits of top-down hierarchies. Every sector, from business to government to nonprofit, has been tinkering with being more open and team oriented, and has been offering more liberty to create and innovate without an instruction manual. We're yearning for more freedom *with*. Yet, despite this greater sophistication and effort, we keep backsliding.

That's because even though we can change our intentions, we can't seem to change our perspective. Here's what I mean: It is common to hear, from both those who truly want to change and those who seem to be speaking through clenched jaws, the same phrase, "bottom-up," thinking that this phrase signifies a real change. It usually follows a pledge to put away their "top-down" ways. But here's the thing: *Bottom-up* is just the same Pyramid perspective, only upside down. And being the recipient of this leader's sloganeering is hardly inspiring when your input is welcomed because you are at the "bottom." We're still in the shape of dependence.

The emergence of each new networked platform and device after the dot-com crash—Google, YouTube, Facebook, and the iPhone, to name a few big ones—offered new hope to unleash energy without hierarchy. Yet by 2012, we weren't feeling better. MIT professor Sherry Turkle studied the impact of these services on all of us, especially young people, and pronounced her verdict in the title of her book *Alone Together*.

Technology has given us independence—freedom *from* hassles and wires and other people's choices—and more efficient lives, but it has largely broken its promise to give us freedom *with* one another to build big things together. Summing up 1989 until now, one could say we are, at our worst, "bowling alone, together." Never have we been so connectable and never have we felt so disconnected.

## THE CONSTELLATION LEAP

What we want (and I think what we need) is interdependence, but the problem is this: The Pyramid mindset will not leave politely. And the Constellation mindset can't be acquired like a new phone or paid for with wine. We might think that interdependence is some state between independence and dependence, but that couldn't be more wrong. In fact, independence is a form of dependence—self-dependence would be a better name—and both involve the same Pyramid mindset.

Interdependence requires gaining awareness of the Pyramid lurking within and then actively releasing it. You must let go of it, along with the security it seems to offer. And, at the same time, you must make a leap to put your faith in the Constellation and in others.

We don't need to worry about the Pyramid mindset ever going away completely, and the truth is we should all be grateful for that. We need it. We need it in times of national emergencies. We need it for go-for-broke, single-minded missions. We need it for contests and drama. But we do not need it for everything. Certainly not for the things we care about most. Yet it's so pervasive that it's difficult to adopt the Constellation mindset and its habits—even if you've got a book like this one.

Our founders put the pyramid on the back of our Great Seal, and we keep putting it in front of our thinking in every realm, from business to politics to the economy. But the leap we need to make is mapped out in a place very familiar to us now. It's right there on our dollar bill, and in the chapters ahead, we'll learn how to make it.

# 2

## CONSTELLATION MAKERS

WHO WON WHEN ONE of the richest companies in the world took on one of the oldest?

That was the question behind Harvard Business School case 396-051, a temporary classic in the category of tech disruption. It's a story of two false leaps and then one last leap into unimaginable success.

The first company in the study was founded in 1760s Scotland, a hotbed of Enlightenment thought but a relative backwater of the European economy. A group of those thinkers believed people were hungry for organized and categorized knowledge about the world. They wanted to create a better encyclopedia and bring the era's explosion of knowledge to a wide audience.

Their key insight was that too often the esteemed French encyclopedias took a given topic and exploded it into bits that were then arranged in alphabetical order. You would find a subject like the human heart chopped up in various sections more like dictionary entries—*aorta*, *blood*, and *chamber* each with its own separate description in a different part of the book. The Scots thought the subjects should be named and grouped more intuitively—reflecting the interconnected way readers would encounter and apply them in the real world.

So, Andrew Bell, a prominent engraver who had been making ends meet by, among other things, stamping family crests onto dog collars, teamed up with Colin Macfarquhar, a book printer and son of a wigmaker, to try to create an encyclopedia of their own. They found an editor in twenty-eight-year-old William Smellie, who had been working as a copy editor at *The Scots Magazine*.

They called their publication *Encyclopedia Britannica* and put it out in one hundred weekly installments. At the end of four years, they bound it together in a three-volume set. By 1790, it was a global hit. Over in the United States, George Washington, Thomas Jefferson, and Alexander Hamilton each had a set.

As Britannica's fame and sales expanded through the 1800s, it attracted the greatest thinkers of the day to contribute voluntarily. Three volumes grew to twenty. When new editions were being prepared—released about every fifteen years—contributors were thrilled to have their names associated with the world's premier trove of collected knowledge.

But the business side was never simple. The product cycle was very lumpy, meaning that the gear-up for a new release required years of investment in editorial staff. Then the company had to hire a sales force to sell the latest edition, while letting go of the editors until the next go-round. Each edition required a big infusion of cash. They kept things afloat for over 150 years, by which time the company had migrated across the Atlantic to the world's busiest market, the United States.

By the 1920s, Sears and Roebuck had taken ownership, willing to put up with the business difficulties because of the brand's prestige. But during the Great Depression, it decided Britannica needed to pull its own weight. Sears put Buck Powell, one of its best corporate operators, on the job. He totally restructured the company. His innovation was that Britannica would always be publishing and always be selling. New editions would arrive every year, whether or not there was a lot of new content to add.

Powell also built a big sales force—2,300 people strong at its peak—to go door-to-door, chasing leads from mail-in forms the marketing department placed in magazines. Finally, in the spirit of consumer predictability, *Encyclopedia Britannica* would now always be the same size. If a new topic demanded four pages, then you had to take away four pages from other topics.

The sales pitch changed too. It started with a question: Are you the kind of parent who is willing to invest in your child's education? It was ostensibly about good parenting, but it was really about guilt. Salespeople made their money by upselling customers to sets with embossed leather covers that cost almost twice what the plain-covered version did. They went to "four walls" training sessions in which they were essentially taught how to box in their customers so they had no choice but to say yes. By 1990, Encyclopedia Britannica reached annual revenues of over $600 million.

The company enjoyed financial success but it also had a secret: research showed that customers hardly ever actually opened the encyclopedias—averaging only once or twice a year. Britannica had evolved from expanding the circle of knowledge to enlighten themselves and others in the 1760s to boxing in readers to buy boxes of books with fancy covers that the company knew they wouldn't read.

## ENTER MICROSOFT

In 1985, Bill Gates began talking to his board about a serious opportunity. Microsoft was taking off based on the growth of the personal computer, having struck a deal to develop the operating system for IBM's machines. But this opportunity centered around the CD-ROM, a new type of removable disk that would soon be making its way into commercial use and could hold the same amount of data as five hundred floppy disks.

Large amounts of digitized text, even entire books, could be stored in one place.

The economics were tricky because buying copyrights for good content was expensive. Plus, people probably wouldn't want to read Tom Clancy on a personal computer. But what about reference books? People might want to clear their desks of those bulky things. Microsoft surveyed the market. Almanacs sold for up to forty dollars. Dictionaries sold for as high as seventy-five dollars. Better. Encyclopedias, on the other hand, were $1,500 to $2,000 a set. The board let Gates give it a try.

Leaders at Microsoft wanted to partner with an encyclopedia publisher, so they went off to pitch the biggest and most prestigious in the business—none other than our friends at Encyclopedia Britannica. Executives at Britannica understood right away what Microsoft would get out of it: the prestige they'd built over two hundred years. But any benefit to Britannica was far too speculative. It was an easy no.

Microsoft went down the pecking order of encyclopedia publishers, collecting nos until they got to Funk and Wagnalls, which sold its *A* volume at grocery stores for a penny, hoping we'd buy the rest via mail order. Unfortunately for Funk and Wagnalls, we almost never did, so it was hard up enough to license out its content to some computer guys.

To make the product, now dubbed Encarta, more attractive, Microsoft engineers realized they could hyperlink to photos and related articles. And they could embed short video clips, like from the moon landing, or audio, like the earliest Thomas Edison recordings.

By then Microsoft was on its way to becoming the richest company in the world and could afford to make investments. Encarta added more video and set up displays at retail stores like CompUSA and Egghead Software. Though the product was high-tech, the pitch was familiar: Are you the kind of parent who is willing to invest in your child's education?

The combination of these insights and a price adjustment was lethal. Year-over-year sales went up 1,000 percent. By the early nineties, Encarta was humming. Soon enough, it was Britannica's turn to come around with hat in hand. It had gone from recording peak sales in 1990 to nearly dead in the water at the hands of Encarta in 1995—the same year that Bill Gates became the richest person in the world. At this desperate hour, Britannica's pitch was the company itself for a bargain-basement price. For Microsoft, it was an easy no, and probably a satisfying one too.

Encarta rapidly built up its editorial team to make more flashy charts and videos and to stay updated with the proliferation of new information—especially because the encyclopedia had expanded into pop culture and business entries. Now the company was padding its lead to make it insurmountable. This is when the Harvard Business School researchers came around to write their case study.

Their verdict was clear. Winner by KO: Encarta.

# JIMMY FROM ALABAMA

Then something unlikely happened at the turn of the millennium. Along came Jimmy Wales, a thirtysomething guy from Alabama who put aside his PhD to become a foreign currency options trader before experimenting with an online startup during the dot-com boom.

Jimmy grew up going to a tiny school run by his grandmother. He was among the outliers who actually read the encyclopedia, in his case the World Book set that his mother had bought for the house. The company sent stickers to customers so they could amend anything they found missing. It may have just been a nice marketing gimmick, but Jimmy eagerly used up all the stickers—carefully adding them to the pages where he found the articles to be incorrect or incomplete or both.

He called his startup Nupedia. He was going to create a high-quality, for-profit encyclopedia online by tapping into experts' passions to teach things to a wide audience, something like what the early Britannica had done, but with a few twists. Essentially, Wales's proposition was this: *We're going to build a better reservoir of the world's knowledge without paying for any content. Oh, and we are not going to charge anyone to use it either. Trust me. I used to trade foreign currency futures.*

One by one, his team reached out to PhDs and other experts, explaining the concept by using the analogy of academic peer review, in which academics check one another's work for free. Many said yes and they built up a respectable initial community. But they soon hit a snag. Given their unorthodox model, Jimmy and his team felt they needed to be scrupulously rigorous about quality and accuracy and therefore had instituted a seven-step review policy before any of the volunteer content would be published. The output was discouraging.

Wales got frustrated and began to write his own article on a favorite Nobel Prize–winning economist he had studied extensively for his PhD. But even he got intimidated about what the peer review committee might say about his piece, so he stopped. After the first year, Nupedia had only eighteen approved articles. Worse yet, it turned out that one had been completely plagiarized.

Then a team member named Larry Sanger pitched a possible alternative. There was a new technology called Wiki, the Hawaiian word for quick, that allowed a group of people to write things together. One person could write a paragraph or even just a sentence. Others could write nothing on the subject but still help edit it into encyclopedia style. Contributors would edit and fact-check one another. No article would have an individual's signature, but all contributions would be attributed on an attached page. Why not use this collaborative method to publish more articles?

Jimmy decided it was worth a try. Nupedia published this

new effort as a companion site called Wikipedia. Lo and behold, it was embraced by the Nupedia community and their friends and theirs. Within a year there were eighteen thousand articles. Jimmy decided that in order to keep quality and participation high, Wikipedia would not sell ads and instead allow voluntary contributions to fund the platform. He wrote a statement of principles that were themselves modifiable by members of the community.

Soon enough, Wikipedia had not just made Microsoft Encarta obsolete; it had developed the biggest knowledge transfer engine the world has ever seen—six-million-plus articles in the English language alone and versions in more than 240 languages.

It's a monumental achievement hiding in such plain sight that we rarely even think about it. When a dispute comes up at dinner we say, "Let's Google it," but most of the time what we're really doing is Wikipedia-ing it. Google's algorithm is designed to take us to the best information on any subject based on previous searches, and that's usually Wikipedia. Try it.

Wikipedia has always had its doubters, but *Nature*, one of the premier journals in academic science, published a study that proved them wrong. It showed Wikipedia to be just as accurate as the old gold standard: *Encyclopedia Britannica*.

So, who won when one of the richest companies took on one of the oldest? Let's turn to Wikipedia itself for the answer.

From the Wikipedia entry for *Encyclopedia Britannica*: "The 2010 version of the 15th edition, which spans 32 volumes and 32,640 pages, was the last printed edition."

From the entry for Encarta: "The MSN Encarta site was closed on October 31, 2009, in all countries except Japan, where it was closed on December 31, 2009. Microsoft continued to operate the *Encarta* online dictionary until 2011."

Looking back now, you'd have to say neither won, but you might also say that, eventually, *we* did.

## JIMMY'S CONSTELLATION LEAP

Buck Powell's Britannica and Bill Gates's Encarta were worlds apart in terms of technology—one old and analog and the other new and digital. But in one key aspect they were identical: their perspective. They were committed to the Pyramid mindset. Experts decided and assigned, locking in power at the top with predictable results.

When Jimmy Wales launched Nupedia he recognized what had been lost in the fight to win encyclopedias. He sought to revive something like the original Britannica but enabled by instant communication and low-cost digital publishing. Yet Jimmy and his team still placed themselves at the top of the system, making it dependent on them and their process. His caution had made him a gatekeeper. His rigorous filtering and fact-checking system blocked all the energy. The implied message was that Nupedia was Jimmy's platform, not everyone's. Despite its new-fangled technology, Nupedia was still a Pyramid.

On Wikipedia, however, users can stand out by expressing individual expertise, and also fit in by being part of a community of people who love information and accuracy. It is forever evolving, with no set destination, perpetuated by people joining together to serve a vision. What made Wikipedia take off was Jimmy's letting go of the Pyramid mindset that defines both dependence and independence. And what made it stick was something that would make Charles Thomson proud: the principles, habits, and sentiments of a Constellation.

Jimmy and his team made the leap.

Unlike Buck and Bill, Jimmy hadn't made profit the single-minded objective. In fact, because he had a Constellation mindset, he didn't have a single-minded objective at all. He had many—and allowed for other people's objectives too. He wanted good information. He wanted to learn about new things. He wanted reading to be engaging. He wanted contributing to be engaging.

But if Constellations aren't single-mindedly in pursuit of profit, can they be profitable? In a word, absolutely. If Jimmy's story shows what can be built without money as the main driver, another leaper reveals how the Constellation mindset has revolutionized money and created the largest commercial organization the world has ever known.

## THE PIONEER

If you don't know the name Dee Hock, you are not alone. He liked it that way. Born in 1929, the year of the stock market crash and Buck Powell's transformation of Britannica, Hock grew up in North Ogden, Utah, forty miles north of Salt Lake City on a thin valley between the lake and the Rockies. It had been only three decades since Mormon leaders formally disavowed polygamy and President Grover Cleveland had granted Utah statehood.

Highly intelligent but too poor for a better education in the city, he learned to rely on his own truth detector and picked up lessons where he could find them, including the wide-open natural world around him. Many years later, reflecting on that time in his life, he said he'd learned that "nature seeks perfection by attention to small things."

Hock was the first in his family to go to college—a two-year associate degree. After graduating, he took a job in Los Angeles to support a growing family. He landed at a consumer credit agency, a sleepy corner of the midcentury financial universe that approved loans to people for things like homes and cars. After some time on the job, he came to a realization made by many before and after: working for a big company can smother the spirit.

His specific critique was with "mechanistic, command-and-control organizations." Large companies viewed humans without humanity, he thought, seeing us merely as parts in a machine. And he thought it was not only soul destroying but also foolish in a business sense. "Purpose slowly erodes into process," he observed. Organizations find themselves in a doom loop of "the doing of the doing."

Hock believed there was a way to allow the organization to ebb and flow naturally based on evolving needs of customers. He thought machinelike organizations were incapable of dealing with the dynamic nature of real life. He believed that biology held lessons about adaptation and evolution that could solve some of the problems.

His company, however, didn't know what to make of Hock's ideas. He beat his quarterly goals but not by the book. In fact, his approach directly contradicted the training manuals for new recruits. He refused, for example, to encourage borrowers to take out as much as they could afford and instead advised caution. Customers borrowed prudently and built confidence in themselves and in Hock, leading to more referrals and customers. It meant more time actively engaging with each customer, but it was energizing.

When his bosses asked him to stop, he was confounded. That would be against the company's own interest. It didn't make sense, so he kept going. Then his company told him he could stop or else stop coming to work. He took option two. This pattern repeated throughout Hock's twenties and thirties until he finally did what most of us are forced to do in the face of corporate realities. He gave in. He took a mid-level job at a mid-level bank in the mid-tier market of 1960s Seattle. He was going to punch a clock for a paycheck and manage younger officers to carefully approve boring loans.

Now, the world of banking looked very different then. For one, banks were much smaller, and they couldn't operate consumer business like checking and savings accounts across state lines, much less across international borders. There were some bigger ones, like Bank of America, which operated in the larger state of California, but despite its name it was mostly constrained by state lines like every other bank.

Except when it came to the relatively small but growing business of credit cards. The business wasn't brand-new in the late sixties. Stores had been issuing credit cards for some years. In fact, you might have had five in your wallet—one for a department store, another for gas, another for, well, another department store. But the concept that you might have one card tied to your bank instead of one for each retailer you frequented, one card that could be used throughout the US, was not lost on the larger banks in California and New York.

Bank of America had been particularly aggressive in California and now it wanted to affiliate with out-of-state banks that could issue cards on its platform, called BankAmericard. That's when Dee Hock got the knock on his door that would knock him' off his clock-punching path. His bosses had signed on to the BankAmericard platform, and Hock, the consumer credit guy, was responsible for managing it.

The Bank of America people briefed him on their game plan. A participating bank like Hock's had two roles: issuing cards to consumers and signing up merchants to accept the card. However, as James Madison famously said at the forming of the Constitution, if we were angels we wouldn't need government.

Very quickly, the less angelic elements of all involved emerged in full force. The system nearly collapsed. Consumer banks like Hock's would hold off on paying the merchants' banks for weeks so they could earn more interest. Merchants' banks would lie to inflate the amounts owed to them. And that was just within the BankAmericard system. The competition from other credit card systems was so intense that some rival card issuers were giving restaurants and retailers new imprinters (those old credit card slide machines that use carbon paper) that would crack the competition's cards in half.

Hock believed that the single-minded nature of the system, fixated on short-term revenue, was running wild. It was threatening the livelihoods of customers, who were being charged high interest rates, as well as the banks' own viability. And so, if past behavior was predictive, it was time for Hock to quit. Maybe there was an even sleepier perch in eastern Washington or back in Utah. But this time, for some reason, he couldn't shake it off. He was certain there was a better way. If the higher-ups were desperate enough, maybe this was the chance to try something new.

Panicked, Bank of America had invited one hundred of its credit card affiliates to a big meeting to work through the problems. Seeing that things were going nowhere, Hock stepped forward. To the others gathered there in Columbus, Ohio, the mid-level banker from Seattle carried no special authority, but hey, at least he was willing to try to untangle the mess. The group agreed to form a committee that would develop a process, and made Hock its chair.

Believe it or not, it's here—where a mid-level manager forms a committee to address process issues—that the story gets interesting.

Hock's committee gathered data from groups of banks that staggered the bosses at Bank of America. Losses were in the hundreds of millions, not the tens of millions as they had previously thought. The system was orderly only on the diagram from the overhead slide at the board meeting. It masked the chaos of what was really happening.

Hock's voluntary leadership earned him greater ownership of the nightmare, but that was okay. He began to believe that this opportunity might be worth it. Having struggled with debt personally as a younger man and having advised his customers against taking on debt earlier in his career, Hock didn't like that the phrase "credit card" gained traction. He saw this work as something separate from, and much more important than, extending consumer credit so banks could make more money. Here was a chance to make a piece of plastic almost like cash (indeed, like the debit cards we carry around today).

This organization would need to be about the future of money itself—a system of exchange based on mutual trust to the benefit of all who participated. And it would need to factor in what he would later describe as "unimaginably complex and diverse institutions and individuals."

Bank of America locked Hock and three others in a hotel across the San Francisco Bay from the company's headquarters to come up with a plan. Hock boiled it down to two big, high-level problems: unrestrained competition among the bigger banks and forced cooperation among the subsidiaries. The team spent each day carefully teasing out problems and possible solutions.

As Hock later told it, he went back to his room on the fourth night and he let himself dream more broadly, "What if . . ." and he wrote down what spilled out. The next morning, he presented a set of principles (paraphrased here) to his colleagues:

> **Rights vs. shares:** Instead of "ownership," participating entities (in this case, banks of any size) could hold a right to participate in the system that could never be taken away or sold to someone else.

**Self-organizing with no centralized power:** Any participant could have equal access to all functions of the system. None could dominate decision making based on size—not even Bank of America.

**Competition *and* cooperation:** Freedom to compete and the ability to cooperate when necessary for the integrity of the system.

To sum it up, if you did these things, you could build a system that was at once durable *and* malleable—joined together in a constant and common purpose with ever changeable form so that ingenuity from any participating bank could never be curtailed and would instead be encouraged and unleashed.

At first, according to Hock, nobody believed that Bank of America would ever give up its power position at the top of the Pyramid and join as an equal. Indeed it balked. But it soon recognized that nothing prevented the other banks from organizing their own network or joining its California rival, Master Charge/Interbank.

Hock convinced the bank's higher-ups that the new organization had the potential to make them much richer in the long run. In fact, he got *all* the affiliates to join within ninety days. Within two years, licenses had been granted in fifteen countries. Four years later, in 1976, the now-global company, based on Hock's recommendation, changed its name to Visa. A name that was at once pronounceable and recognizable in many languages and stood for empowering individuals to freely travel and associate.

We now take cards like this for granted (and resent those banks that gouge us with high interest rates), but the Visa company and platform is another quiet miracle hiding in plain sight. To best appreciate it, think about the system we have for protecting our identities around the internet. If you're having trouble imagining it, that's the right answer. There isn't one. Instead, there's just a mess of passwords that we constantly update and forget for each place we visit. Dee Hock solved this challenge with something we guard just as preciously—our money. Today, Hock's system handles sixty-five thousand transactions per second. It's a Constellation of more than forty-six million merchant locations and fifteen thousand participating banks in more than two hundred countries, for a total volume of $11,000,000,000,000 (that's trillion) annually.

## HOCK'S CONSTELLATION LEAP

In that moment of inspiration in the hotel, Hock performed a Charles Thomson and synthesized the principles for a new Constellation. Taking what he'd learned and gathered from banks and colleagues, he made the leap from deep inside the Pyramid of dependency.

His concept of rights vs. shares was something like the difference between democracy and old European feudalism. Liberty wouldn't be bought or dictated—it was an unalienable right, as Jefferson, Franklin, and Adams might say. When protected, this right unleashed the energy of cooperation and competition—a diverse and evolving ecosystem like Hock had observed in the Utah desert.

Hock had a favorite word that I'm sure baffled many listeners. *Educe.* It is hiding in plain sight in the root of a word we use daily: *education.* It means "to bring or draw forth something already present in a latent or undeveloped form." By removing dependency on Bank of America and by developing a system that protected against the chaos of thousands of independent actors, the banks—and merchants and consumers—educed energy from one another. They became truly interdependent.

Dee Hock became wealthy. Visa is one of the ten most valuable public corporations in the world as of this writing. But at age fifty-five, Hock left the company and became something of a philosopher. He had seen so much technical progress in his lifetime and knew that the pace of change was speeding up but also that we were stuck in outdated, static models (our Pyramid mindset). The result, he observed, is that "our expertise became the *creation* and *control* of constants, uniformity and efficiency, while the *need* has become the *understanding* and *coordination* of variability, complexity and effectiveness."

In his autobiography, he reminds us that it's tempting to point fingers in frustration at institutions like governments and corporations, but Hock stresses that these institutions are not separate from us. They are a reflection of us. Here is how he puts it: "In truth, there are no problems 'out there.' And there are no experts 'out there' that could solve them if there were. The problem is 'in here' in the consciousness of you and me."

The rest of this book is devoted to showing in greater detail how, led by geniuses of the Constellation, we can get "in here" to make a new mindset and then, in turn and with others, make a big impact "out there."

# 3

## MAKING THE MINDSET

THE 2005 *New York Times* obituary for Peter Drucker called him the twentieth century's most influential thinker to leaders of corporations, nonprofits, and governments. In fact, Harvard Business School published a list of the two hundred most influential leadership gurus and then asked these two hundred to identify the person who had the most impact on their thinking. In other words, the researchers compiled a new list—the gurus' gurus—and Drucker was number one. Drucker himself never liked the guru label, though. Instead, he saw himself as a "social ecologist" in the tradition of Tocqueville. Yet toward the end of his life, Drucker wrote an essay revealing that he had his own guru too—the gurus' guru's guru, if you will.

This person had been the most sought-after name on the business speaker circuit in the 1920s and, according to Drucker, "the brightest star in the management firmament." Her name was Mary Parker Follett. Warren Bennis, founder of the Leadership Institute and also on the top gurus list, acknowledged that "just about everything written today about leadership and organizations comes from Mary Parker Follett's writings and lectures." Yet only one decade after this ur-guru's death in 1933, all memory of the famous talks and writings had essentially vanished. This towering figure, lamented Drucker, had "become a 'nonperson.'"

It's a tragedy. Because she had already revealed and articulated what later had to be stumbled upon and intuited by the likes of Jimmy Wales and Dee Hock—namely, the power of giving away power. Fragments of her insights remain in top-selling leadership books today, but the Pyramid mindset keeps obscuring the core concept. Recovering her teachings is a first step in shifting our mindset so that we can make Constellations ourselves. And as she'll soon show us, it can start right away at tomorrow's meeting.

## MARY PARKER FOLLETT: THE GURUS' GURU'S GURU

Mary Parker Follett was born outside Boston in 1868 at a time of faltering reconstruction for both the country and her family. Follett's father, Charles, had fought for the Union in the Civil

War from beginning to end and was suffering from severe alcoholism and what we would now call PTSD. Meanwhile, Mary's mother, Lizzie, was for long periods a single mother, estranged from her husband yet expected by the strict social conventions of the day to live off his meager income, even though her own father, a banker, was quite wealthy.

From a young age Mary felt the tension between official authority—with its clear rules about everything from what to wear, how to speak, and whom to marry—and the world of her own heart and eager mind. She was expected to accept that her father should be cast out of polite society, but when Charles was sober he was the parent with whom she felt a soulful connection. She was expected to stay home and help her beleaguered and sometimes bedridden mother, but she was the smartest kid in town with ambition to burn. She was expected to plan her life around a future husband, but she was never even attracted to boys.

During her school years, her father finally quit drinking. She'd seen how hard he had struggled to quit. And how often he'd failed. She'd also seen how none of the attempts by authority figures—his military commanders, local ministers, or his in-laws—had been able to change her father's habits. Each person had, in one way or another, condemned his behavior from on high—demanding that he fall in line, stop sinning, or pull himself together.

What finally worked was something very different. A

temperance speaker had come to town who, unlike the typical ones, didn't spin tales of miraculous redemption or stoic self-reliance. Instead, he talked in detail about his own pain and failures and how close to death he'd come. At the end of the talk, Charles publicly signed his name to a commitment to stop drinking and later joined a fellowship group of pledge signers that met regularly and took turns telling their stories like the speaker had. It finally stuck for Charles. He'd saved himself through others.

And that lesson stuck with Mary too. She earned a scholarship to one of the new private high schools that admitted girls, and she graduated at fifteen, titling her senior essay "The Schoolmate as an Educator." It was about how her peers had taught her just as much as her teachers. On graduation day, Mary was asked to give a speech. Her mother and father were back together again and were seated in the audience. Informed by a senior-year elective course in the emerging field of "mental science" and inspired no doubt by her father's recovery, her speech described how things not yet imagined or not yet even present in "the world of fact" can be created with the "all-powerful agency of the mind." In essence, the speech was about the power of changing one's mindset to change the reality around you.

The Annex at Harvard, the precursor to Radcliffe College, accepted Mary as what they called a "special student," a label for people who commuted to school, had to work part time to support their studies, and wouldn't be taking the traditional linear progression of the normal "matriculating students." She took this freedom to continue her eclectic courses combining history, political science, economics, philosophy, and mental science.

Mary found an intellectual soul mate in a star professor, William James. At this moment James was simultaneously co-developing the first truly American-born philosophy (pragmatism) and turning mental science into a proper discipline by literally writing the textbook (*The Principles of Psychology*).

James had suffered from acute depression and suicidal thoughts. He had helped popularize the term "Americanitis" for the sense of purposelessness that many felt after the Civil War: the life of striving, concern, and confusion about how to function in an increasingly urbanizing, commercializing, and industrializing country. Then he discovered the seeds of his philosophy and his profession by trying to cure himself.

He had tried on for size, but ultimately rejected the established, all-sorted-out-in-advance belief systems, whether religious or scientific. For James, these systems demanded dependence on dogma and left no room for him to use the power, purpose, and potential he felt within himself. At the same time, he resisted the logical and trendy alternative, "self-reliance," made famous by his godfather, Ralph Waldo Emerson. Emerson said, "Nothing can bring you peace but yourself." James had spent enough time brooding by himself to know that radical independence wouldn't work for him. He knew he mattered and he knew he wasn't the only one who mattered. So, he arrived at another idea: What if I could change the world around me but only through and with other people?

He discovered that his mindset toward others made a big difference not just in his own perception but also in the world around him. To be sure, how he chose to think about gravity didn't change whether the apple fell from the tree. But for many things, what he thought and felt mattered a lot in how things turned out.

For instance, think about something you care about greatly, like your relationships. Let's say you calculate that your trust and love ought to be withheld from someone until they show you beyond a shadow of a doubt that they love and trust you first. Chances are, they will never give it to you. On the other hand, if you begin the process, without any assurances, of extending your trust and love to that person, the odds go way up that it will be returned.

Love and trust are mutual. Many, many other things we care about—laws, manners, prices, and really the bulk of our daily experience—are co-created by all of us and improved or degraded by what we bring to them. Therefore, James believed, the pattern we set and the tone we take with others are immensely more important than any argument we might make. So much so that a year before he died, James gave a graduation-style speech to the women of the Annex and said that all of human history is a matter of whose "pattern and tone" we choose to adopt and emulate. He admitted that "'tone,' to be sure, is a terribly vague word . . . but there is no other" because "by their tone are all things human either lost or saved." It all hinges on tone. Our whole democracy, he said, hinges on tone.

Mary had grown up just miles from the birthplace of the Revolution. The adult grandchildren of John and Abigail Adams lived just down the street. Her father helped save the Union in the Civil War. All that Americanness and still Mary had never felt very free. She knew that even in a supposed democracy, there was no shortage of formal and informal power being lorded over others. She also knew from her father's fellowship society, her high school classmates, and the electric environment at the Annex that another kind of power could be summoned among peers for very different ends. So, when it was time to write her senior thesis, she set her sights on the nature of power in the seat of that supposed democracy, Washington, DC.

Her work looked at the thirty-nine men who had held the job of Speaker of the House of Representatives, all the way back to Charles Thomson and his similar role as Secretary. The Speaker leads without any constitutionally defined or orgchart power over anyone else, yet this job was perceived as second only to the presidency in terms of power. Not content just to review the historical record, Follett insisted on interviewing all living Speakers in an attempt to tease out their patterns and tones and find out what made leaders succeed or fail.

She concluded that the most effective leaders neither relied on hierarchical positional power nor fell back on their personal powers (say, being good debaters or gifted public speakers) but rather developed a creative blend of techniques involving both formal and informal power that she called the "unwritten practice." The successful leaders made their colleagues in the often convoluted committees and subcommittees feel like they were generating the power together in a group in response to the demands of the situation at hand and not feel like pawns in someone else's game.

When she turned in her thesis, her professors at the Annex were astounded at the achievement and helped her publish it. Today, we might call it a landmark leadership book. It made a big splash. Unpretentiously titled *The Speaker of the House of Representatives*, it got reviews from *The New York Times* and *The Times* of London and a rave one from an up-and-coming New York politician serving as a police commissioner named Theodore Roosevelt.

## MARY PARKER FOLLETT FINDS HERSELF (IN OTHERS)

If Mary had been a man, the reception of her book would have amounted to a career-making launchpad, earning her a professorship at a place like Harvard. But that path was not open to women. Even at the Annex, her professors hadn't been required to teach female students and had to volunteer to do so. Frustrated at this lack of opportunity, Follett considered just retreating up to the woods of Vermont to pursue an independent life of writing.

One benefit of that plan: she could live there in peace with the woman who had become the love of her life—the person cryptically referenced in her book's dedication "to I. L. B." Isobel Louisa Briggs, a school headmistress twenty years her senior, wanted a life with Mary just as much, but refused to allow Mary to retreat to the woods. Mary, she insisted, ought to do more than merely write about the nature of power.

The United States was changing fast, especially with the huge waves of immigrants who were filling cities like Boston, and these newcomers were challenging the customs of the American Constellation. Follett got introduced to the progressive reformist crowd of upper-middle-class women who had just developed a new social reform innovation: settlement houses where reformers could live and work in immigrant communities side by side with immigrants. They gave her funding to start a debate club in Roxbury, a poor neighborhood of Boston brimming with newly arrived immigrant families. She helped young people train for jobs.

She soon began to see that her progressive peers had a blind spot. Their own strict conventions about what was proper didn't allow them to see where human energy was being created and where it was being killed. The reformers' stated goal was to integrate families into American life, and their programs had indeed proved effective with women and children but had persistently failed to attract a key constituency: dads. Follett sensed that something about the tone of the settlement houses didn't make the fathers feel welcome. So, in that same exploratory spirit she had taken with her book on power in the House and no doubt reflecting on her own father's struggles, she asked, Where do these dads feel comfortable? Where might they feel free from condescension and judgment?

Follett saw that men felt comfortable in saloons and union meeting halls—places where "boss politicians" of the "machine" were perceived to be in control. For that reason, progressive types who advocated for "good government" wanted to get rid of those places. Follett saw the bad, but also lots of good. People were getting to know one another, opening up about their struggles. Real relationships formed there. So, when the main funder of Follett's work asked her to chair a new group called the Anti-Saloon Committee, Mary accepted with one condition: that they call it the Committee on Substitutes for the Saloon.

She wasn't into abolishing things that were alive and attracted people to them. She wanted a place where women, men, and children all felt equally welcome. That's when she recognized there already was such a place—the public school. What if schools kept their doors open in the evenings too? Neighbors could make of these spaces what they needed—gathering places for purposes as varied as political meetings, stamp-collecting societies, and basketball leagues.

The idea of giving away space and power to these new immigrants made many suspicious. Machine bosses didn't want these spaces to rival the saloons' influence on voters (remember, only men could vote). School committees worried they would get hit with more costs. Settlement house reformers worried that their turf was being threatened. Follett didn't run from any of these misgivings. Instead, she embraced the tension and conflict. She didn't let one of these groups dominate or be dominated— she kept them all at the table.

Soon, she was instrumental in spreading the changes from one school in Roxbury to many throughout Boston and then around the country—in her lifetime over 240 cities adopted what was called the community center movement, New York City alone had five hundred.

Meanwhile, her success with job training got her appointed to a women-in-the-workplace board and then to Boston's newly created minimum-wage board, which dealt with increasingly bitter labor disputes. This work brought her to a table with business owners and their workers and gave Follett her first glimpse into what we would call "corporate culture." Yet another unglamorous committee filled with conflict that would turn many of us off, but she was onto something.

Here was a chance to see two groups at a table where each—employers and employees—truly needed the other and unlike do-gooding upper-middle-class reformers who could walk away if they got bored or frustrated, these people would have to figure *something* out. This was a chance to explore what had become her passion—how small, diverse groups of people with a dizzying array of different and diverging hopes and fears can try to work together to make something more impactful than they could alone. It was in this unlikely place that Follett made the realization that launched her to worldwide fame as a leadership guru.

## MAKING THE CONSTELLATION MINDSET

For years, she suspected there was a better way of using power to get more done. Now she knew it. Her eyes had been opened to the growing ravages of the Pyramid mindset—forcing people to conform to set roles or else casting them out if they didn't fit in—and she had to do something about it.

Nearly two decades after her first book, Follett, approaching fifty, decided it was time to write again. Americans needed a guide for how to reconcile their Constellation with the mass industrialization that was marking the dawn of the twentieth century. In the introduction of *The New State:* she emphasized the high stakes: "Our political life is stagnating, capital and labor are virtually at war . . . because we have not yet learned to live together." She realized she had been living her whole life for the same core idea, and now, she told Isobel, she was willing to die for it.

From the founding of the Republic to the founding of an after-school program in a public school, from the House of Representatives to a settlement house—it all hinged on how we reacted and interacted in small groups. Follett knew from both observation and participation that human energy could be created and kindled or smothered and killed based entirely on what mindset we each brought to the encounter. How you could create spaces where each person could at once stand out and fit in. How could we create unity among radically different people with divergent priorities without mandating uniformity? Follett wanted to revive the Constellation for a new time.

Her first order of business after this epiphany: end the debate club she had started many years before. No longer did she want to teach young people to use words as weapons with a goal of "winning." Instead they must learn something else—"that all our work in life is interdependent."

Next up for reconsideration: meetings. She had attended thousands of committee meetings in every realm of civic life. She had a PhD in meetings. Like all of us, she knew how dreadful they could be. But that's because we were doing it wrong. Meetings, she realized, are where our most meaningful work ought to happen. Not just planning for growth, not just planning for change, but growing and changing right then and there.

She developed very clear principles for how things ought to go. Follett believed that meetings have four possible outcomes, but *only one* is good:

**Bad outcome #1: Acquiescence.** Just give in and let someone else (the pushiest or the highest-ranking person, generally) have their way. This means you have not done your duty to bring your whole self and your wishes, worries, and experiences to the group.

**Bad outcome #2: Victory.** You "win." You are able to prevail upon everyone else the idea you had coming into the meeting by bullying or charming or cajoling others into acquiescing to your vision. But in the process, everyone else loses their ability to contribute.

**Bad outcome #3: Compromise.** Most of us think compromise is a good outcome, but compromising is just the practice of hammering out partial acquiescence from all participants. No growth or group investment takes place because no one leaves satisfied.

**Only good outcome: Integration.** Integration is her word for the final option and only happens when all members of a group make a new thing together. This new thing is truly yours as an individual *and* truly the product of the group. You are in it. It is of you. And your individuality is not diminished as a result. It is enhanced. This outcome is not a melting pot. It is not a salad. It is a Constellation.

Integration, not compromise, is what Charles Thomson managed in channeling his three committees for the final Great Seal. It's what Jimmy Wales did when developing principles for Wikipedia along with its growing community. And it's what Dee Hock enabled on behalf of Bank of America and the other large and small banks in the system.

A Mary Follett meeting is the micro unit of what interdependence looks like. Follett knew, from observing energy kindled and created or smothered and killed everywhere she looked—from the House of Representatives to a settlement house—that we can unlock energy and become more than the sum of our parts. This creation of energy and power through one another requires that "instead of shutting out what is different, we should welcome it because it is different. . . . Every difference that is swept up into a bigger conception feeds and enriches society; every difference which is ignored feeds *on* society and eventually corrupts it."

And for Follett, interdependence wasn't some passive state of interconnectedness—it was an active verb and a choice. She believed that small groups were "the indispensable means for the discovery of self by each man." And the Pyramid mindset squanders the potential energy of difference by forcing everyone to be either dependent or independent. Dependence drowns out each individual's potential. And independence suffocates individual identity because it doesn't contribute to anything bigger or anyone else.

Like others who made the Constellation leap, she knew that a set of principles, habits, and sentiments for interdependence needed to be articulated in a way we could each apply in our own lives.

We can boil it down to three expectations we should take into every meeting:

**Expect to need others.** Enter with the intention to make differences and diversity fruitful in order to make something together.

**Expect to be needed.** Bring your whole self to the meeting. Ask and answer hard questions to the best of your ability and pursue them wherever they may lead in an atmosphere of trust.

**Expect to be changed.** Yes, you need to (as we say today) bring "your truth" to the encounter. But Follett insists you have a reciprocal obligation to allow that truth to be affected by others. You should expect to leave a meeting not quite the same person as when you entered.

If we succeed at integration, then we have *made something*. You are part of it and it is part of you, but—and this is important—you have not lost yourself in it. You have given power to the larger co-creative activity, but your own power isn't diminished. It is increased. Same for everyone else.

Some indigenous people of the north have umpteen words for "snow," and the ancient Greeks famously had at least four words for "love." Well, Follett had seven terms for the co-creation that happens in these meetings: interweaving, interpenetrating, interlacing, interknitting, intermingling, reciprocal response, and activity-between. She had plenty of words she hated too—like *absorbed* and *assimilated*—because they made it sound as if people were losing their individuality when they should do the opposite. You must make yourself *more you* in the process.

There's a helpful phrase that has taken hold in corporate HR departments in the past decade: *diversity is a fact; inclusion is a choice.* The point is that diversity is all around us and always has been, and acknowledging diversity is a first step but not enough. Inclusion is an action—what we *choose* to do with the diversity. We need to actively include that diversity into our companies, our teams, our meetings, and so forth. Mary Follett would tell us we shouldn't stop there, though. That's not nearly enough. Inclusion gets the right people to the table and *then* the hard work begins. What we need to do is spark the energy and connection between people to make something that is bigger than any individual. She might amend the phrase as follows: Diversity is a fact; inclusion is a choice. *Co-creation is the work; interdependence is the promise.*

## FOLLETT BECOMES A GURU

Business leaders in the 1920s were among the first to see how Follett's insights applied to them. "Business" as a respectable profession was just beginning to take shape. Socially, business had been considered grubby work compared with law, medicine, and architecture, although great fortunes were beginning to change that. As the size and complexity of their companies grew—one made textiles and the other made, say, confections—

owners and executives recognized that they had the same management headaches. A small group of progressive businessmen (they were all men) who loved Follett's work invited her to New York City to give a lecture at the first-ever professional development seminar for national business leaders.

Their common challenge was how to bring together large, diverse groups to produce good results. In the previous decades, business leaders had (eventually) gotten the memo that the old model of one all-powerful business owner wielding arbitrary power and barking orders at subordinates (think Scrooge) was both bad for employee morale and bad for business. In fact, when Follett hit the equivalent of today's CEO speaking circuit, the dominant trend in this new field of business was something called "scientific management."

Its founder, Frederick Taylor, wanted to "depersonalize" business—take out all that Dickensian drama and bring in experts to essentially mechanize the process of work. He encouraged organizations to closely monitor factory workers in order to weed out any inefficiencies in their body movements. His ideas took hold, requiring ever more managers to watch the workers. In the decade after 1910, the number of supervisors grew at more than double the rate of wage earners. The result was that workers felt "at the bottom level of a highly stratified organization"—what we might call a Pyramid. Taylor had predicted that the progress from his ideas would be so great that any bickering between labor and management would disappear. As it happened, just the opposite came to be.

Follett certainly didn't want a return to Scrooge—she knew firsthand how crushing arbitrary power from on high could be—but she saw that "depersonalization" had real human costs too. It was intensely personal to those losing power on the factory floor to men in white jackets with clipboards who monitored their every move. Intensely personal to those who felt like they were so many cogs and wheels in a machine. Those feelings should all count even though they can't be measured to Taylor's scientific specifications.

Instead, Follett called for *re*-personalization—to bring the right kind of struggle into each encounter. In what became her standard presentation, she encouraged leaders to allow all members of the team to share their views and study the problem at hand from many angles, with each person bringing their knowledge to the table. If you did this with your teams, then you could avoid the traps of arbitrary personal power and the twin danger of depersonalized power—you would still have power, but it would be what she called "power-with," not "power-over."

Her "power-with" lecture became a hit—a phenomenon akin to giving a TED Talk that goes viral—and she was asked to speak all over the country. She gave the keynote address in 1925 for the Executive Conference Group, speaking to leaders of the country's largest companies, like R. H. Macy, MetLife, General Motors, Standard Oil, and AT&T. She was invited to

London by the dean of the London School of Economics to play a leading part in their national conversation too.

Then, at the height of her fame, came the stock market crash of 1929. Businesses were no longer hoping to improve; they hoped just to keep existing. Survival eclipsed all else. Follett was struggling just to survive too. She had recently lost Isobel to cancer, which, according to biographer Joan Tonn, was like experiencing her own death. Then, on December 18, 1933, she succumbed to cancer herself at age sixty-five.

There was no obituary for her in *The New York Times*. No mention of her decades later when Harvard Business School published their gurus' gurus list with Drucker at the top. In fact, according to Drucker, nearly all memory of her famous talks and writings was also dead within a decade. He felt this total erasure couldn't be fully explained by the rank sexism of this period. He wrote, "The only explanation is that her ideas, concepts, and precepts were being *rejected* in the 1930s and 1940s," those Pyramid years of monolithic responses to national emergencies— the Great Depression, WWII, and the Cold War.

To point out just how much perceptions of power had changed since Follett's death—from the excitement of creating boundless new "power-with" opportunities to the grim, zero-sum hoarding and lording of a finite amount of power— Drucker noted that the top-selling book just three years after she died was *Politics: Who Gets What, When, How.*

## NEAR MISSES

As decades passed, Follett's work was rediscovered every so often, but it never seemed to take. Yet we can see her finger-prints all over many popular contemporary management ideas. In 1989—the year the wall came down and the Web went up—one of Drucker's protégés published the year's bestselling business and self-help book.

Stephen Covey sought to bring a fresh way of thinking and behaving to a new generation—an approach grounded in hab-its. *The 7 Habits of Highly Effective People* was perfectly timed with this new era of freedom and its anxious twin, uncertainty.

The book is essentially broken into two sets of habits: first, those that help you progress from being dependent to being inde-pendent, then those that help you progress from being independ-ent to being interdependent. Covey considered the second set the most important. Let's take a look at his habits of interdependence:

- Think win/win: find mutually beneficial solutions
- Seek first to understand, then to be understood: listen with empathy
- Synergize: combine strengths through teamwork

We can see Follett in each of these, and just as in her time, the ideas garnered huge interest. *7 Habits* stayed on top of the charts the following year. And the next, and the next. Not only is it the bestselling book of all time in its categories, it *still* sits atop the current bestseller lists today.

However, a decade and a half after publication, it had become clear to Covey that, although we were easily becoming personally independent, we were having great difficulty with these habits of interdependence. In an appendix to a fifteen-year anniversary edition, Covey notes that he wishes he had been more clear that interdependence is ten times more important—and ten times harder—than independence. That same year, Covey published a book called *The 8th Habit* with the single goal of reinforcing the point that "interdependence is a higher value than independence." Looking around us another decade and a half later, it seems we're no closer. What's so hard about these habits? What's the problem?

The Pyramid mindset is so insidious that even Stephen Covey hadn't realized it was still lurking within.

Consider this: The goal of the first set of habits, progressing from dependence to independence, is called a "private *victory*." The goal of the second set of habits, moving from independence to interdependence, is a "public *victory*." And the first habit of interdependence (#4 in the book) is "think win/win." Victory, victory. Win, win. The Constellation mindset says win/win is a losing formula.

Yet winning is the aspect of the Pyramid mindset that is the hardest for most of us to let go of.

Let's try something.

If I ask you to tell me the opposite of winning, you'll of course say "losing." But what if I press further and ask you to tell me the opposite of winning-and-losing? Nine out of ten of us will say something along the lines of "sitting it out" or "not playing" or "not participating." Okay.

If the opposite of winning-and-losing is sitting it out, then it logically works in reverse too. If you're not sitting it out, that means you are out there in the business of winning-and-losing. You are active and involved and "in the game."

But now let's try a few other questions:

Are you winning most of your friendships?
Is your relationship with your mother a win/win?
In the course of your marriage, can you describe your
   spouse's greatest win?

Most important activities in our lives—the things we *do* with our greatest sense of participation and involvement—are not winnable. You don't win a marriage or a family or a friendship, although if you try to win them you could very well lose them. Yet "win thinking" has permeated all aspects of our lives.

I remember some clichéd but well-intentioned advice delivered by a successful businessman at a graduation ceremony for my daughter. It is so well known I bet you can fill it in: "Life is not a sprint; it's a _____." Everyone nods along. But sprints and marathons are more alike than they are different. And think about the assumptions here: (1) life is a race to be won or lost; (2) you go in one set direction; and (3) you run it all by yourself. This is our Pyramid mindset at work—binding us to a set destination with a predictable course and blinding us to our need for those all around us. If someone wins, someone, somewhere, must lose. This is why Follett, at age fifty, canceled the debate club that she had started twenty-five years before.

What *is* the opposite of winning-and-losing? How about playing? How about engaging? Or better yet, how about making big things together? This is the mindset Follett wanted us to bring to every meeting and to every day at work: expect to be needed, expect to need others, expect to be changed. The Constellation mindset draws its power from those things we do with our greatest sense of participation and involvement, those things we care about most and can never win: relationships.

The success of *7 Habits* spawned a whole consulting empire and a leadership center devoted to bringing the message beyond the bookshelf and into the workplace. See on the next page how Covey illustrates the private and public victory model.

Notice those triangles, or, as I see them, pyramids? I cannot help but look at this picture and see the Pyramid mindset infiltrating what Covey hoped would be a guide to forming Constellations.

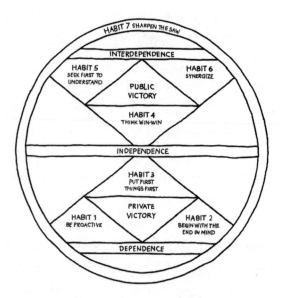

The only other business book to really rival Covey's in terms of sales has been Jim Collins's *Good to Great*, which came out in 2001.* Collins instinctively rejected the kind of CEO worship that was at its height in the late nineties and focused on companies instead of individuals. He and his team of researchers set up a "management laboratory" and rigorously analyzed data on thousands of publicly traded companies to discover secrets to success based on anything but the person at the top.

But then his researchers found something that surprised them. The data suggested that the leaders of all the "great" companies had something in common. They were deeply humble

---

* I loved the book, and it's one of the books I have given away to others most.

and even shy. They rarely talked about themselves. These leaders had something else too: an incredibly intense determination and ambition, but not for themselves. It was for group achievement.

It sounds kind of familiar, doesn't it? These leaders who can stand out *and* fit in. These leaders who create space for others. These leaders who aren't your typical "winners." They nurture connections by educing, to use Hock's strange word, the energy of everyone around them. Collins calls them "Level 5 leaders" and says they "never aspired to be put on a pedestal." Yet that's precisely where Collins puts them—at the top of a pyramid, like this:

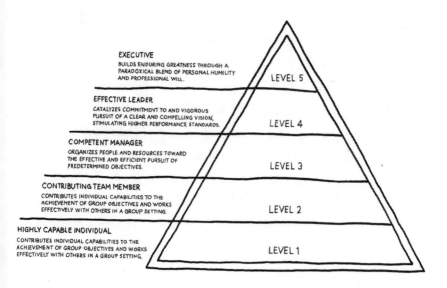

EXECUTIVE
BUILDS ENDURING GREATNESS THROUGH A
PARADOXICAL BLEND OF PERSONAL HUMILITY
AND PROFESSIONAL WILL.

LEVEL 5

EFFECTIVE LEADER
CATALYZES COMMITMENT TO AND VIGOROUS
PURSUIT OF A CLEAR AND COMPELLING VISION,
STIMULATING HIGHER PERFORMANCE STANDARDS.

LEVEL 4

COMPETENT MANAGER
ORGANIZES PEOPLE AND RESOURCES TOWARD
THE EFFECTIVE AND EFFICIENT PURSUIT OF
PREDETERMINED OBJECTIVES.

LEVEL 3

CONTRIBUTING TEAM MEMBER
CONTRIBUTES INDIVIDUAL CAPABILITIES TO THE
ACHIEVEMENT OF GROUP OBJECTIVES AND WORKS
EFFECTIVELY WITH OTHERS IN A GROUP SETTING.

LEVEL 2

HIGHLY CAPABLE INDIVIDUAL
CONTRIBUTES INDIVIDUAL CAPABILITIES TO THE
ACHIEVEMENT OF GROUP OBJECTIVES AND WORKS
EFFECTIVELY WITH OTHERS IN A GROUP SETTING.

LEVEL 1

Collins acknowledges that he doesn't know if these leaders actually follow steps one through four to arrive at Level 5. He is quick to point out that he and his team don't exactly know how leaders develop Level 5 skills and habits and perspective. He says he wishes that he could publish a "10-step process to become a Level 5 leader," but he doesn't know how and fears that such a list would trivialize the talents. At the end of *Good to Great*, Collins reveals that he and every member of his team were so moved by the experience of writing about these leaders that they hope to one day become as great, but they fear they might never achieve it.

Follett would tell them that what they seek cannot be found in a "management laboratory." What Follett tells us (and what Jimmy Wales and Dee Hock showed us) is that the magic isn't isolated in a particular leader. It exists between the leader and the people in the group—it's mutual. You cannot start as a "highly capable individual" and climb the Pyramid in orderly steps (as the five levels suggest) and hope to achieve Level 5 greatness. It's not a solitary race to a set destination. It's a leap—to, with, and through others.

There's nothing wimpy or touchy-feely about these ideas. "Cooperation is going to prove so much more difficult than competition," Follett said to a group of top CEOs during one of her famous keynote speeches, "that there is not the slightest danger of any one getting soft."

And, as we shall see, the most quoted leader of the twentieth century agrees with her.

# 4

## LETTING IT GO

By 1940, seven years after Mary Parker Follett died, FDR's fight against the Depression was succeeding but not yet won. Across the Atlantic, though, many felt all was already lost. In Britain's "darkest hour" the Nazis were sweeping across Europe, and bombing was underway in London. The American public was still battle-weary from World War I and didn't want to be involved in another offshore conflict. Winston Churchill thought that America entering the war would be the only hope of stopping Hitler from ruling all of Europe. Roosevelt thought Churchill was probably right and understood that staying out would likely mean facing a powerful, fascist foe for generations to come, but his hands were tied.

FDR's ambassador to the UK, Joseph Kennedy (JFK's father), had been sent over to London in 1938. The rumors at the time were that FDR sent him so that he wouldn't challenge him for the next Democratic nomination; Kennedy was rich and well connected. For his part, Ambassador Kennedy didn't seem overly concerned about hiding his ambitions. He had a replica of the Oval Office built at the American embassy in London at his own expense. He was just the sort of leader Jim Collins was so wary of.

In the darkest hour, Kennedy said privately that "England is gone." He had sought a meeting with Hitler "to bring about a better understanding between the United States and Germany." The Nazi ambassador, Herbert von Dirksen, told his bosses that Kennedy was "Germany's best friend" in London and that he "fully understood our Jewish policy." Kennedy himself said he was "for appeasement one thousand percent." Finally, Kennedy said out loud and on the record, "There's no sense in our getting in [the war]. We'd just be holding the bag." He advised Americans in Britain to flee the country. The British, he said, were a "lost cause."

This moment marks one of history's great what-ifs. What if Hitler had been appeased and American public opinion had been pandered to? Speaking strictly politically, it was the low-risk move. But, as fortune would have it, FDR decided to stall for time. He wasn't ready to take on Hitler, but he also wasn't ready to give him more propaganda from his own ambassador. Roosevelt recalled Kennedy from his post and sent a man named John Gilbert Winant in his place. This turned out to be one of the war's critical decisions, if also one of its least remembered, because it drew the first connecting line in the Allied Constellation that would win the war. It would soon be known as the Special Relationship.

## SETTING A DIFFERENT PATTERN AND TONE

Winant was an unconventional choice. He was from the opposing political party as the president, and he was not your usual political type. He was not smooth. He was shy by disposition and he had a stutter. He ran for governor in conservative New Hampshire on a platform that included increased civil rights for African Americans, a decrease in the workweek (forty-eight hours) for women and children, an increased minimum wage, regulation on big banks, and an end to capital punishment. He won. Then he won reelection twice.

From the moment he stepped off the plane in England, Winant dedicated his whole being to making the British cause America's cause. In a move that had never occurred before nor since, King George VI personally met the ambassador's train on arrival. Winant immediately made his position clear: "There is no place I'd rather be at this time than in England."

That quote ran across the front pages of all the papers the following morning. At Winant's welcome luncheon, Churchill told him, "You, Mr. Ambassador, share our purpose. You'll share our dangers. You'll share our anxieties. You shall share our secrets. And the day will come when [we] share together the solemn but splendid duties which are the crown of victory."

Winant refused to live in the fancy ambassador's residence. Instead, he took a small apartment near the embassy. He walked the streets of London in the late-night hours after bomb attacks, helping to pick up the rubble and asking people—air raid wardens, firemen, rescue workers, families in the shelters—what he could do to assist. He wrote and called daily back to Washington, urging FDR and his team to join the British people in standing up to Hitler. He and Churchill developed an extremely close relationship. They spent many days and late nights together at the prime minister's official country house, forty miles from London.

That's where they were, talking after dinner in December 1941, when word came over BBC radio that Japan had attacked Pearl Harbor. Churchill jumped up and pronounced, "We shall declare war on Japan!" and ran off to call Parliament. He believed this would finally entice America to come to England's aid. Winant ran after him and said, "You can't declare war on a radio announcement!" Winant said he would call Roosevelt. With the two of them listening into the earpiece, FDR told them what they'd been wanting to hear for so long: "We are all in the same boat now."

The moment was the culmination of desperate, war-weary, faith-testing work together. Winant and Churchill's reaction was one of pure joy that Hitler might be beaten. They danced around the room together. There would be time soon enough to be sobered by the attack and the conflict before them.

The next summer, a new kind of threat to the war effort arose. Coal miners in the northeast of England were on strike, threatening Britain's war-making capabilities. When Churchill discussed the crisis with the leader of the opposition Labour Party, they agreed on a solution: send Gil Winant. Such was the trust and respect this foreign official had created with leaders from both parties.

In his speech in Durham, Winant never once used the word *strike*. He didn't try to win a debate or even have one. He let go of all that. As if following Follett's instructions on the mindset required of a leader and how to create power-with and not power-over, Winant equated the battle against fascism with the fight for social democracy. "This is not a short-term military job. . . . We must solemnly resolve that in our future order we will not tolerate the economic evils which breed poverty and war." The next day, the conservative paper headline read WINANT TALKS, STRIKE ENDS. The Labour paper hailed it as "Gettysburg in Durham!!!"

## CHURCHILL AND TRUMAN AND ANOTHER LOGO

When the war was won, true to Winant's words, Britain did set itself on a new path of social and democratic reform, as did

America across the Atlantic. The voters threw Churchill and his party out of power, FDR died, and Winant went home. Churchill was left feeling dark and lonely in what should have been his hour of triumph.

Invitations poured into his office from American universities and institutions of all kinds, but Churchill declined them all on the grounds that nobody really wanted to hear from a has-been. Then one day his daughter noticed that one invitation in the pile on his desk had come in an unusual envelope—from tiny Westminster College in tiny Fulton, Missouri—and had an extra handwritten note at the end. It read, "This is a wonderful school in my home state. Hope you can do it. I'll introduce you. Harry Truman."

Churchill accepted the new president's invitation. Not only did Truman repeat his offer to introduce Churchill, but he also invited Churchill to come along for the train trip from Washington, DC, to Missouri. Churchill's spirits revived instantly. Here was a chance to keep the pattern and tone he had set with Winant and FDR going and growing with Truman and the American people.

At the start of the journey, Truman found Churchill alone, loitering outside the president's special train car at Washington's Union Station and inspecting the painted presidential seal on its side. Now, after the Depression and World War II and the rise of a powerful executive branch, it looked something like the Great Seal, but, tellingly, the Constellation had been removed altogether. Forty-eight stars, representing the states, now made up a decorative circular border. Truman confided that he had even toyed with the idea of adding a lightning bolt to symbolize his country's new nuclear capability.

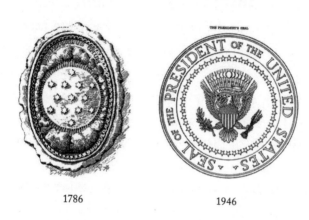

1786                    1946

The two men spent the next twenty-four hours together in a tricked-out Pullman car designed like a room in a men's club. They talked politics, Churchill worked on his speech, and the staff joined them now and then for poker. Churchill good-naturedly and consistently didn't win. The train went straight through, day and night, deep into the heart of America. It made its one and only stop for fuel in Springfield, Illinois, where Churchill reportedly looked out the window with reverence— "The home of Lincoln," he said out loud to no one in particular. His mother was American and he knew his history. Upon finally arriving in Fulton, Churchill and Truman drove an open convertible down a cheering main street to Westminster College.

# ONE IRON CURTAIN VS. MILLIONS OF SPECIAL RELATIONSHIPS

The riser in the college's gym was modest, but the stage was enormous. Word had gotten out about the subject of Churchill's speech and that it would be some sort of wake-up call. Press had gathered, and arrangements had been made for the speech to be broadcast internationally. Churchill felt the world was repeating many of the same mistakes that led to the rise of extreme ideology after World War I. Specifically, he worried about Stalin stoking communist revolution in Europe—a controversial point of view in March 1946 because Stalin had so recently been a wartime ally.

Churchill's remarks are remembered as the Iron Curtain speech because of his vivid metaphor for Stalin's plan to consolidate power across Eastern Europe, but that was not what he came to say. He was not there to sound an alarm so much as to summon the West to a new cause. Great strength would again be necessary to resist a gathering threat. In the nuclear age, the future of humanity depended on it. So what was it that he prescribed?

Would the best way to face down a monolithic consolidation of power be to consolidate and centralize our own? To fight Pyramid with Pyramid, to use our language? No. The great lion of defiance and victory believed it was time to put the Constellation first again. To prevail against the threat of the "iron curtain," he prescribed a "special relationship" between America and Britain, and, more important, *special relationships* between Americans and British. And between other democracies around the world too.

His answer was to meet the power of armies and dictators with the energy of free people, together. He believed that our allied response must be grounded in the special relationships of individuals who had fought side by side, and who had prayed on separate sides of the Atlantic for the same thing; who understood the specific inheritance of freedom dating from the Magna Carta to the Declaration of Independence to Victory Day; and who understood the role of the citizen and the responsibility each had to take ownership of a common destiny.

If we did the hard work of forming these relationships and preserving these connections, millions of them, old and new, official and unofficial, then together they would form lasting bonds—"sinews of peace," he called them. "The Sinews of Peace," he underscored for his audience in Fulton that day, was the title of his speech and its purpose.

This speech was not a call to arms. It was a call to form Constellations. He feared that Americans might want to sit it out in isolation again after two world wars or, just as bad, remain perpetually poised for war, with the Western world dependent on American military might. Winning wasn't the end—it was a prologue to a new and different kind of work. "We aim at nothing but mutual assistance and collaboration" to increase "each other's . . . powers." Remember that Churchill had foreshadowed this at the welcome luncheon for Winant when he said that with victory would come "solemn but splendid duties." It was time to let go of the Pyramid mindset. This would require "faith in each other's purpose, hope in each other's future, and charity towards each other's shortcomings."

## SPECIAL RELATIONSHIPS AND ROUTINE TRANSACTIONS

From that day forward, the Special Relationship has remained in use as the name of the US-UK alliance. The term has been the source of great pride over the years, and also much cynicism. Every decade or so pundits declare that the Special Relationship is dead, only for it to reassert itself as the most critical connection in the Western Constellation. It has been the linchpin of global security since World War II.

As US ambassador to the UK from 2013 to 2017, I would get a close-up view of it. But a few days before I moved with my family to London to take up that posting, I got an email from a British friend. He wrote, "A bit of advice (worth what you paid for it): Don't be one of those people who bangs on about the so-called Special Relationship—it's a cliché and not true anymore anyway."

Two weeks later, on August 29, 2013, the British Parliament took a vote on the question of whether to authorize the use of force to help the United States in a potential conflict in Syria. It didn't pass. This is what ran on the front page of the highest-circulation newspaper of the country the following morning:

"Death Notice: The Special Relationship. Died at home after a sudden illness on Thursday, August 29, 2013, aged 67. Beloved offspring of Winston Churchill and Franklin D. Roosevelt. Dearly loved by Margaret Thatcher, Ronald Reagan, John Major, George Bush Snr, Bill Clinton, Tony Blair and George W Bush. Funeral to be held at The French Embassy. . . . No flowers please."

That friend wrote again: "Well done, Matthew. The Special Relationship—seven decades in the making and you've killed it in less than seven days."

I struggled to articulate in the press interviews that followed why the latest death pronouncement of the Special Relationship was just as premature as all the previous ones had been. My staff put the phrase in speeches and it was met with head-nodding from half the room and eye-rolling from the other. A sure sign of a cliché is that people either disagree or agree immediately—no thought necessary. If I was going to use that phrase, I wanted to mean it—and build mutual understanding of what was meant by it.

It was time to unpack it, so to speak. That's what you do in couples therapy when the relationship is feeling stale or the energy is evaporating. But instead of using "I statements" or uninterrupted listening, I borrowed from the world of business therapy, also known as management consulting.

I drew a two-by-two grid.

On the *x*-axis, we have *special* on one end—in the sense of "unique" but not necessarily in the sense of "delightful"—and its opposite, *routine*, on the other. The *y*-axis runs from *transactions*—about things—to its opposite, *relationships*—about people. The quadrants look like this:

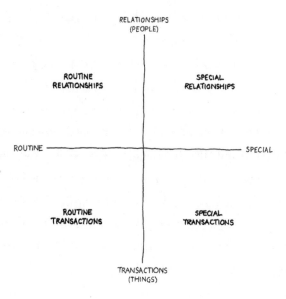

Let's first look at *routine relationships* and then at *special transactions*—the upper-left and lower-right quadrants. It turns out they are instructive and form a certain pattern and tone when taken together.

In *routine relationships*, we engage with each other but view each other in terms of function. We are the jobs we perform for one another, and at our worst, we treat each other as parts of a machine or merely a means to an end. When you exit a plane, the flight attendant says, "Thanks for flying with us, thanks for flying with us, thanks for flying . . ." You can hear the exact same phrase said to the three people in front of you and the three behind you. No wonder Southwest Airlines has enjoyed so much success deviating from this well-known script with humor. In the routine relationships quadrant, we're made to feel like we don't stand out.

In *special transactions*, we feel like we are being forced to conform to some standard that doesn't account for who we really are. The most maddening special transaction is when you are handed the dreaded clipboard at the doctor's office and required to fill out the same eight-page health questionnaire you know you must have completed a dozen times in previous visits. In this quadrant we are being recognized as unique but in the worst bureaucratic way. "Aren't I already in the system?"

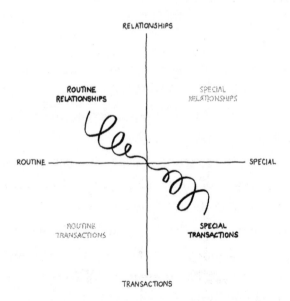

So much of the worst of life at the office is spent in these two quadrants. And as we bounce back and forth each day, week, month, and year, we form a vicious cycle, a doom loop of dependency. We are dependent on systems and the conventions within them. We feel we must fit in to work within the system or be left out, with no real power or agency. No surprise that this is where the great workplace satires like *The Office*, *Office Space*, and *Parks and Recreation* get their best material. And the sharpest ridicule is saved for the so-called leaders—the Michael Scotts, David Brents, Bill Lumberghs, and Leslie Knopes.

In each case, there is *frustrating friction*. You might reasonably say it would be best just to avoid the friction altogether and automate everything possible. And that's exactly what we try to do.

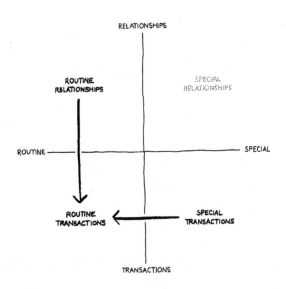

We want to turn these awkward routine relationships and special transactions into routine transactions—to push them down or left on the grid. We want to automate things and get rid of frustrating friction, like the form at the doctor's office.

This is true of so many things in our lives. Automation brings us a certain kind of independence—here we are again. We achieve freedom *from* dealing with people in these awkward-quadrant situations. This is satisfying—but only up to a point and only temporarily. There's a catch. And a cost. The problem is that achieving "freedom from" misses the power-transfer potential (as Mary Parker Follett illuminated). There is no connection.

A small example: Social media platforms can easily prod you when someone in your network has a birthday. With one click you can automatically send them a happy birthday message. We know what it's like to receive those. Nice but not memorable. Imagine that instead you received a text from a friend that is two days late for your birthday and says, "I am so, so sorry I forgot your bday. Would love to bore you with excuses, but mainly just want to say I am thinking of you on this special day." How much better would that feel?

We're using our incredible technology, even our connectivity technology, to create ever more friction-free lives. So much of our brain power and investment are going into technology to help us achieve that goal, but our two-by-two grid shows us that this is actually the opposite of what Churchill believed would save the world. Churchill told us we need to seek special relationships. We must go up and to the right.

When we find ourselves in the awkward quadrants, we must try to get out by humanizing and empathizing, not by automating and replicating. The special relationships quadrant is not friction-free. There's friction here, but it is *fruitful friction.*

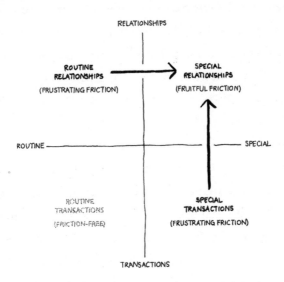

Turning routine relationships and special transactions into special relationships is the essence of Constellation power creation. It means creating space for our humanity and expecting to need others, to be needed, and to be changed. This inevitably raises new issues to factor in—how to bring in more perspectives and create room to discuss personal issues more often and in different ways—but facing and welcoming this new friction generates energy instead of depleting it. That's what Follett did in her committee meetings, and that's what Winant did when engaging the strikers.

And if you are feeling a bit wary, this isn't just Churchill's advice from seventy-five years ago. It's the same conclusion reached by one of the most exhaustive internal studies ever performed by one of the most successful companies of the twenty-first century. In 2012, Google began a two-year study to determine what makes, in a nod to Stephen Covey, a highly effective team. They found that the distinguishing factor was interdependence. The more interdependent the team, the more it was a *real* team capable of high levels of effectiveness and not a mere work group. But that was just the beginning.

The researchers collected data from 180 teams and analyzed over 250 attributes, everything from skill sets and group dynamics to personality traits. What was the most important factor of an effective, interdependent team? Was it the percentage of high-performing individuals? A charismatic team leader? A consensus-driven leader? A diverse team, or a homogeneous one? Turns out, none of those. When it finally came time to analyze the data, what mattered most was what the researchers dubbed "psychological safety." These were the teams in which the relationships were strong enough that mistakes weren't held against people and it was okay to bring up hard stuff, to disagree, to ask for assistance, and (to quote Churchill) to show "charity towards each other's shortcomings." In other words, the best teams were the ones whose members could form special relationships.

## BLOOM LOOPS

The Google study discovered what Churchill knew from a lifetime of experience—that if you invest time and energy in the special relationships quadrant, something magical happens. The connection and power generated from fruitful friction carries through into routine transactions, where energy is retained until fruitful friction is required again. Fruitful friction leads to a sense of frictionlessness, and back again, in what I like to call a *bloom loop*.

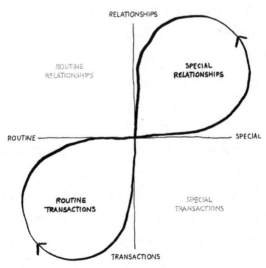

Take an example from home life: a school-day breakfast in a family with young kids. Each person comes to the kitchen and knows their role and routine—make coffee, toast, lunch—and it may appear to an outside observer like so many routine transactions. Very little is spoken as the family members weave in and out of each other's way through the meal and out the door. But that ballet of breakfast is earned by the drama of the dinner table, where misunderstandings, tears, arguments, laughter, awkward silences, banter, interruptions, confessions, and fruitful frictions of all kinds are worked through.

In the UK, I saw a bloom loop every day. American and British diplomats, soldiers, and government employees interacted as though they were virtually from the same country. The British press were always quick to declare the Special Relationship dead after a rift of some kind, but they had it exactly wrong. It was our ability to disagree with affection that created fruitful friction and allowed the bloom loop to live on.

So I thought a big part of my job was to create dinner tables, so to speak, inviting fruitful friction. To that end, I gathered a group of young British and American activists, journalists, and diplomats who had expressed special interest in and frustrations with the internet—privacy and surveillance and monopolies and so forth. And then, because so many leaders come through London, I was able to set up a session with Vint Cerf, who co-invented the internet.

The seventy-something-year-old Cerf put everyone at ease immediately, didn't give a lecture, and addressed their frustrations head-on. Halfway through the discussion, he realized these young leaders kept talking about the internet as one big monolithic thing. But it isn't one thing, he explained. It's millions of things. And then he interrupted himself to say that it originally wasn't even made up of "things" at all. In the early days, *internet* wasn't a noun (singular or plural); it was a verb. The computer servers were dubbed *hosts*, which gives us a clue about how human and relationship-driven the internet was intended to be.

Getting two computers to communicate wasn't the clever part of what Cerf and his co-inventor, Bob Kahn, created—that had been around for a while. But it was very cumbersome. You would connect two computers and then those computers would be locked in, unable to do other things while they were connected. It was a mode of dependence. Cerf and Kahn's insight was to unlock all this potential for different networks to connect to form sinews of communications, so to speak. It would require owners of computer networks to take the leap with them.

They set about talking to their colleagues at other universities and research institutions, one by one, about the idea of connecting their networks in this new way. It was a bold request, asking people to take the leap of faith and open up their networks. "We would call people up and ask them, 'Would you like to internetwork with me?'" That was the verb. "It was like asking someone to dance," said Cerf.

The special relationships that Cerf and Kahn formed at the beginning created a human protocol on top of the computer one they had developed. Initial friction up front (asking to "dance") then allowed for friction-free interchange and the formation of voluntary groups that, in turn, could spring into action when new frictions arose, like how to handle the explosion of domain names when the World Wide Web took off. Bloom loop magic in action.

Cerf had no idea what it would become. He closed our session by reminding the next generation that some had said no when he asked them to dance (like the French, who had a centralized system called Minitel). His internet protocol was deemed "unreliable" in the computer science lingo of the day because it didn't lock in a guaranteed, dedicated connection between the computers—there was uncertainty at its core. Yet that series of "unreliable" connections grew to form the most reliable network the world has ever known.

Whether it is "sinews of peace" or an "unreliable network" or Hock's committees or Wikipedia's volunteer editors or Follett's community centers or the leaders Collins called "Level 5," something causes the characters who make these special relationships to keep coming back to the table. They don't do it for selfish reasons. They don't do it for selfless reasons either. And they don't do it to score a win/win. Something else is going on.

# FREEDOM TOGETHER

One of the world's foremost Constellation leaders in the realm of philanthropy is Lynne Twist. She worked with Mother Teresa and with communities in sub-Saharan Africa, Bangladesh, and Sri Lanka on the problem of widespread hunger in a world of abundant resources. Twist's book, *The Soul of Money*, has been key in challenging my own Pyramid mindset (more on that in the next chapter), and I got to meet her not long after she had made a career change, shifting from her anti-hunger work to a new vocation in the Amazon rainforest.

I asked her why she had made the switch. Had she felt the Amazon needed more help than the fight against global hunger, or had she burned out? She answered with a story. A few years back, she'd heard about the Achuar people of the Amazon. They'd tried their best to avoid the encroachment of global culture and business, but deforestation came to them. She felt a calling to drop everything she was doing and be of service. She undertook a four-day trek to pitch her offer of assistance to the tribal chief. When she arrived, exhausted, she was offered tea by the fire with him.

Through an interpreter, she explained why she was there. The chief listened carefully and then said, "I think I understand." He considered his response for a moment. "If you are here to help, please leave."

Oh no, she thought. That didn't go well. But then he continued, "But if you are here because you feel your liberation is bound up with ours, then stay—let's work together."

*If you are here to help, please leave. If you are here because your liberation is bound up with ours, please stay.* A declaration of interdependence if there ever was one. That distinction—that way of putting it—clicked immediately for Twist. Only freedom together brings the power to heal, and it always heals both.

Not surprisingly, Follett learned that same lesson in her time. She called it "reciprocal freedom." Freedom together can and should happen not just between two people but between groups at any scale—like between Churchill and Winant, Winant and the miners, Churchill and Truman, and the millions of people who Churchill hoped would form special relationships across the Atlantic to create bonds of peace. As Follett wrote, "To free the energies of the human spirit is the high potentiality of all human association."

## THE HABITS NEEDED TO KICK THE HABIT

Alcoholics Anonymous was founded in 1935 when a stockbroker helped heal a doctor as a part of healing himself. Now the organization is in 180 countries and has 130,000 chapters serving millions every day. Bill W. (that's AA nomenclature and how he's remembered) had tried to give up drinking in all the standard ways of the time—quitting cold turkey, checking himself into a hospital, and so on.

On a business trip to Akron, Ohio, he felt the urge to drink. Desperate, he went to a phone booth and found the number of a priest to cold-call. He said to him, in effect, "I am an alcoholic and the only way I can save myself from drinking is talking to someone like me so that I can try to save them. Do you know any alcoholics?" The priest didn't know anybody directly but knew someone who did—a woman named Henrietta who had been unsuccessful in her attempts to help an alcoholic friend in crisis, Dr. Bob Smith. Henrietta made the connection and the two men met up at the doctor's house.

Bill W. confided in Dr. Bob about his struggles. It was the first time Dr. Bob had heard the story—so familiar to him—of a fellow struggler. They agreed to help each other. They decided they would start with six steps that Bill W. borrowed from another organization. They later expanded the process into the twelve steps that are now well known.

It's a story about the pattern and tone of finding freedom together. The same pattern and tone that saved Mary Follett's father. Tellingly, we have all heard of the twelve steps, but less well known and equally crucial to the success of AA are the "twelve traditions" that Bill W. and his team developed for how a group works within itself and how groups work with one another. The traditions aim to preserve freedom together, without tilting toward complete dependence or complete independence. One principle states that AA is to remain nonprofessional; another says that the organization should never be too "organized." The traditions also discourage unbridled individuality: the last tradition reminds participants that AA strives toward principles and not personalities. The members take the "anonymous" part seriously and conceal their last names, not out of shame but as a precaution against too much self-aggrandizement.

*Alcoholics Anonymous: The Story of How More Than One Hundred Men Have Recovered from Alcoholism*, published in 1939, became known as the Big Book. Right before publication the co-authors panicked because a few of their fellow addicts had fallen off the wagon and they feared that the subtitle of their book might not be technically true and skeptics would pounce. They were right to be concerned that the establishment wouldn't take them seriously. The American Medical Association's review stated: "The one valid thing in the book is the recognition of the seriousness of addiction to alcohol. Other than this, the book has no scientific merit or interest." The Pyramid mindset usually misses what cannot be measured and seeks to analyze individuals in isolation. That's why it is so ill-equipped to guide us with relationships. The magic is what happens in between. The book, it should be noted, has been translated into sixty-seven languages, and when AA printed the thirty millionth copy in 2010, the organization sent that special milestone copy to the American Medical Association.

The co-authors couldn't control the reviews. But they could continue counting every person and watching the pattern repeat with and by each new member.

It's no secret that the Iranian government is no great admirer of American books and ideas. Iranian leaders ban all kinds of books that include Western ideas, from Dante to Dan Brown. But they don't ban the AA book. In fact, they print it and distribute it to mosques throughout the country. Why? Because freedom together not only works; it has the power to spread its own power.

# 5

# LETTING IT GROW

TAKE A LOOK AT the two photos below. On the left is Barack Obama in the summer of 2007. On the right, he's being sworn in as president in the winter of 2009.

How does a man named Barack Hussein Obama go from a cornfield in Iowa, twenty-seven points behind in an eight-

Cornfield in Iowa, summer 2007

Inauguration Day, winter 2009

candidate race, to being sworn in as president in front of two million people only eighteen months later?

Astute observers and participants have written books on the subject. Some call our attention to the leader in both photos, a gifted speaker gaining his voice and confidence. Others want us to focus on the crowd: first, a small group of elderly white voters, then a huge and diverse audience. Still others point out that the most important factor isn't shown in either photo—namely, the economic meltdown that happened during the general election.

Of course, all three of those elements—the candidate, the citizens, the political and social environment of the time—played a role. But to my mind the cause of that result wasn't any one of them in isolation. Nor was it purely a synthesis of all three. No, it was something even more important and fundamental.

The Constellation mindset won that campaign by promoting a very particular pattern and tone, as we'll see in this chapter. It's there between Obama and the group in that Iowa cornfield and that group of groups in Washington, and it can help us understand the role of leaders, followers, and external factors in forming Constellations and putting them into practice so the pattern grows.

Notice I said that "the pattern grows" and not how we can "grow the pattern." Most of us use *grow* in the transitive sense.

We say we grew the business, we grew flowers, we grew the economy. Grammarians have relented on this usage over the years, but traditionally *grow* was an *in*transitive verb that didn't take an object. You can plant and cultivate and fertilize corn, but really, the corn grows itself. I would urge us all to recognize what we can—and can't—control as we talk about how Constellations grow and what patterns they follow.

## ASK EVERYONE

In 2004, the Democratic presidential nominee was John Kerry. He is a distant cousin of mine. How distant? I once doodled a simple family tree for a British friend. She looked up and said, "Ah, yes. We have a name for that in Britain: strangers." Fair. Still, it helped me get an internship with him when he was a freshman US senator and I was a freshman in college in 1989. I wasn't thinking a lot about the wall coming down or the World Wide Web going up. My chief memory is that I got trained to operate a device that held a pen and could perfectly copy his signature.

Fourteen years later, in 2003, he declared he was running for president. I called to ask if there was anything I could do to help. Unfortunately, I got the answer I dreaded: fundraising. I feared I would be terrible at asking people for money. I was.

My New England upbringing had trained me to never talk about money, politics, or religion. Fundraising in my adopted home state of Kentucky required all three.

I pledged to raise $10,000 despite my discomfort. My typical pitch went something like this: "I am sorry to bother you, but I am trying to fulfill my pledge to help John Kerry run for president and am hoping you could help me by giving two hundred fifty dollars toward my goal of ten thousand dollars." After two months, I had raised 30 percent of my goal—from my wife, my mother, and myself. I didn't call the campaign to say I quit, but I stopped trying.

That's when I met Lynne Twist, who told me that story about how "helping" doesn't help—it's either freedom together or "please leave." Well, it wasn't the only story she told me. She was in my home city of Louisville for an event hosted by my mother-in-law, Christy. Christy knew about Twist's fundraising prowess; it was no accident that we were seated together at dinner. I told her about my struggles and confided that I had essentially dropped out.

She listened and then shared that she used to be like me but had figured something out. She said it was all laid out in her book, *The Soul of Money*, but perhaps my eagerness and exasperation made her offer me a shortcut. She said the steps were pretty simple—there were just three—so I got a napkin and wrote them down.

Here's what she said and what I scribbled:

1. Money is like water. When it flows it heals. When it's stagnant it kills.
2. Only ask people who want to use money for a cause greater than themselves.
3. Ask everyone.

Thinking about letting money flow helped me reframe donations as something for neither hoarding nor "helping." Instead, money could be a means for, as Twist says, healing—for freedom together. And the seeming incompatibility between numbers two and three tripped me up as it did many, and as she intended. Her point is that *everyone* wants to use their money for a cause greater than themselves. That cause might not be your cousin or your candidate. Or your political party or even politics at all. But it is something. And by asking them to give, you are helping them make their money flow.

After my conversation with Lynne, the "nos" didn't hurt. I saw each one (and there were plenty) as a potential "yes" to some other candidate or cause the person cared about. That counted for something in Lynne Twist's view, which I had now adopted as my own. And each "yes" or "maybe" wasn't about me alone or helping me with my pledge; it was about making something together for a higher purpose. I got much better at fundraising. I asked everyone.

Based on this success from what was deemed the unlikely locale of Louisville, I was then asked to be part of a new fundraising tier. It was made clear to me that it wasn't the top tier—there were many tiers evidently—but it was "up" from where they perceived me to have been. Right from start, the pattern and tone of this DC-based fundraising apparatus was significantly different from what Twist encouraged.

In this capacity, I worked on a big event under one of the leaders who had been at the top tier for many campaign cycles. Right before the event, which we knew was going to be a success, he gathered a small group of us who had raised the most money in his dining room and handed us each a present—neckties with the campaign logo on them. There were ten of us. Only two were men.

You know how the campaign ended: Kerry lost and Bush won a second term. Now we know that Kerry would later become one of our most accomplished secretaries of state, but after the election, things were pretty dark in my worldview for a while.

## LIGHTING UP THE ROOM

It's a law of modern politics that if you raise money for someone, your name and number will land on the target list of every candidate in the party. Two years later, I was still screening out all calls from area code 202. But one day my wife, Brooke, cautiously answered an unfamiliar number beginning with 312.

"Matthew, you're going to want to take this one," she called up the stairs. I did. It was Senator Obama.

"I see here how much you and Brooke did to raise money for Kerry," he said. I appreciated the lack of pretense. He was looking at a printed-out spreadsheet during what is innocuously referred to as "call time" for senators. His tone conveyed warmth along with a subtle sense of the absurd that the American political fundraising system brings out in thoughtful people. "I'm helping the Democratic Senatorial Campaign Committee," he went on. "And I'm in charge of the middle of the country, including Kentucky. Would you be interested in helping support the DSCC?"

"Well, not really, to be honest." He laughed. I went on, "But I would love for you to come to Louisville, and if doing a DSCC fundraiser is the way to make that happen, then okay."

He had given his famous "red states and blue states" speech two years before at the Democratic Convention, and he was already being hotly discussed as a presidential contender. He said he would come, and I decided to press my luck. "Fantastic . . . Just one more thing: people like you don't come through Louisville every day, so would you mind doing a quick event for free when you come since most people here obviously won't be able to come to our fundraiser?"

"Sure, we can do that." And then he added, laughing, "Just promise not to put anyone weird on stage with me." He was true to his word and so was I. As planned, we raised money at the high-dollar fundraiser. But the free event, which we had thought might be a fairly small gathering, blossomed into five thousand people filling our minor league baseball park, Louisville Slugger Field.

Obama stayed the night in Louisville so he could meet Muhammad Ali the next morning, but just before their appointment, we learned it would be delayed a few hours. I figured he would want to catch up on work and offered my office for some private time. He had another idea instead.

"I know it's last-minute, but do you have any friends who couldn't afford to come to the fundraiser last night?" he asked. "Or any friends who aren't Democrats? It would be great to invite them over and just hear what's on their minds." Living in Kentucky, we had plenty of Republican and Independent friends.

We quickly got a group of ten or so gathered around a conference room table. He spoke a little, but not much. He went around the table and asked people what they were thinking and feeling. He followed up to make sure he understood what each of us was trying to say. He wrote down a few notes every now and then and wrapped up the conversation with a short summary of what was said and how he viewed some of those issues. Then it was time to meet The Greatest and then get to the airport to head back to Washington.

On the way to the airport, after visiting Ali, I checked my voicemail. It was full of calls from the friends who had been around the table. Each said how impressed they were by Obama.

That wasn't surprising, but they also went out of their way to say what an inspiring speaker he was. That was strange. I had been paying close attention. He really hadn't spoken much at all.

I answered a call from a friend who couldn't make it to the meeting, and she asked expectantly, "Did he light up the room?" I had to think about that for a second. I knew what she meant. We all knew politicians like that, but the answer wasn't so simple. Yes, the room got lit up, but no, he didn't light it up in the way my friend meant. Not like a big beam of light that you are attracted to (or maybe stunned by). Instead, he got everyone to switch on their own light somehow.

Mine too. Which helps explain my spontaneous parting words to Senator Obama when I dropped him off at the airport: "I hope you run for president. And if you do, I will drop everything and volunteer full time."

## A CONSTELLATION TAKES SHAPE

When Senator Obama called a few months later to say he would be running, my pledge became a job. I said we would pull together another fundraising event—for his own campaign this time—in Louisville. Many of the volunteer fundraisers I had met on the Kerry campaign had by then already committed to other candidates—John Edwards, who had been Kerry's VP candidate, or Senator Hillary Clinton or Senator

Joe Biden or others. When I was called to Chicago to form a "national finance committee" in a small basement meeting room of a hotel, the deep freeze over the city that day contrasted with the warm, outsiderish camaraderie of those of us joined together for the beginning of something.

A well-seasoned volunteer kicked it off by asking what type of fundraising tiers this campaign would have. Obama's answer was simple: none. He dispelled any notion that we should keep our group exclusive. He wanted the finance committee to spread. In fact, he needed it to spread. He closed the session by saying, "Thank you for being here and being part of this. And when we meet again, if we are not at least three times as big and in need of a much bigger room, then we are doing something wrong."

I returned to Louisville with that mission in mind, starting with the small circle of us who had teamed up on the events a few months earlier. We decided to do a typical fundraising dinner, soliciting the maximum donation per person, and also a second event for those five thousand from Slugger Field and others who wanted to give twenty dollars to be a part of something bigger than themselves.

There wasn't a template for this in-person "low-dollar" event. It wasn't done in campaigns because it was considered inefficient: 1,000 people × \$20 = \$20,000. You could much more easily get one hundred donors to give the maximum \$2,000, and raise ten times the amount.

But having witnessed the excitement that evening in the ballpark, I felt we had an obligation to try something different. Our organizing team went to find thirty people who had been there and ask them if they each might find thirty more people to commit to twenty dollars. I started with Ryan, a talented local filmmaker whose day job was at The UPS Store down the street from my house. I had come to know him well during the Kerry campaign when I would send in checks and donor forms to campaign headquarters every week.

I asked him if he could find thirty friends to invest at twenty dollars, and he said he had no idea but would try. I checked in the next day and he said, "Done—can I try for thirty more?" That pattern repeated with the other twenty-nine volunteers. Our first venue held 1,800 but we quickly oversold that. We printed make-shift tickets and picked a new venue. Then we shot past the 2,400-person capacity of that one. With the event only two weeks away, we settled on a 3,200-person venue and hated having to cut it off. Things were going well with the high-dollar event too, which had sold out at two hundred people. I was feeling good.

Then I got a call from Michael, the fundraiser staffer who had been at Senator Obama's side for that original 312 call. He said he had good news and bad news. The good news confirmed that Obama was coming on February 27. The bad news was they had time for only one event. It would be the high-dollar fund-raiser. We would have to cancel the low-dollar one.

I hung up and told Brooke the news. She shared my disappointment, but not my resignation. "You need to get on an airplane and go to Chicago and make your case," she told me. I explained that I didn't want to be one of those annoying fundraisers who complain and make it about themselves. She insisted, "If they say no, then this isn't the campaign you thought it would be, and you shouldn't devote so much time to it."

She was right. It had taken me only one election cycle to realize how easy it was to stifle a campaign's original magic. Uninviting and refunding those 3,200 people would turn their support into a stagnant pool of wasted potential energy.

I flew to Chicago headquarters that day. Michael helped me track down Obama's campaign manager, David Plouffe, in the hallways of the sparsely furnished Chicago HQ with its coffee-spill-camouflaging carpets and unused, unloved filing cabinets stacked against the walls. It was on this unlikely battlefield that I made my stand. We would cut into the time at the high-dollar fundraiser to allow time for both, I explained.

David listened respectfully but not exactly enthusiastically. "I hear you, but no. We're gonna do rallies in the summer when we need to build excitement and crowds and they can give online later. Right now, in this first quarter, it is all about the 'money primary.' So we'll do your rally later."

"This isn't a rally," I persisted. "We already did the excitement part this past September with the five thousand at the ballpark before he announced. This is a *fundraiser.* They already got to hear him—now they want to invest."

"Yeah . . . but no." He was firm.

I stared at my shoes and the sad carpet for an awkwardly long time. David finally said, "Sorry, man. You look really bummed out. What's going on?"

"I'm trying to figure out how to give back the thirty-two hundred tickets and the money," I explained.

"What?" he said. "You mean thirty-two hundred people have *already* signed up and committed to invest?"

"Yeah. Twenty bucks each."

I could see his expression change. It still wasn't that much money for a presidential campaign. But he now recognized that the event wasn't about what we might call the special transactions needed to hoover up online donations later, but that something more powerful was happening—thousands of special relationships were forming.

"Well, go for it then!"

We did, and the event became a template for the in-person, low-dollar fundraisers the campaign rolled out across the country.

## THE CONSTELLATION GROWS

Several months later, as Obama got more momentum, the campaign leadership asked me to co-teach a fundraising seminar in Chicago for one hundred other volunteer fundraisers from around the country. We laid it out like a workshop, placing ten volunteers each at ten circular tables, trying to mix people from different regions. We asked the groups to talk about what they most wanted to get out of the daylong session. Eight tables said the same thing: we want talking points so we can win the argument on why to support Obama instead of Hillary Clinton. Once the other two tables heard that, they changed their answers and said they wanted the same.

Inspired by what I'd seen around my conference room table in Louisville and bolstered by success in emulating this pattern and tone with my own fundraising over the past months, I asked for a show of hands. "How many of you like to lose an argument?" No hands, of course. "If nobody likes to lose arguments, why do we convince ourselves that we're in the argument-winning business? What will we actually win?"

This sparked a lively discussion and we talked as a group about the way it usually works in campaigns: you *arm* yourself with talking *points* so you can *blast* your *target* list of previous donors, *snag* a few by calling them, and ultimately, through all this activity, succeed in *landing* a few max-out donors.

Borrowing a metaphor from business writer and blogger Seth Godin, I summed up what I thought made this campaign different: Notice how all these words call to mind hunting or fishing. If you bring a hunting mentality, you get hunting results. If ten deer are standing under a tree and you fire at one, the best case is you get one and nine run away. It's just bad math. If, instead, you approach fundraising like farming, the math changes. You are planting seeds. Not all will take root, but those that do will bear fruit and more seeds. Our job is to spread the seeds.

Sensing this was too metaphorical for some, we turned to actual numbers. We had a slide that showed Hillary Clinton's campaign fundraising from the first quarter of 2007, just a few months before. At launch, the Clinton campaign had roughly 250,000 names in its database from her Senate runs and from former president Bill Clinton's campaigns. By the reporting deadline at the end of March, they had converted fifty thousand of them into actual donors.

That's great shooting. Anyone who has ever done direct marketing knows that converting 20 percent is beyond impressive.

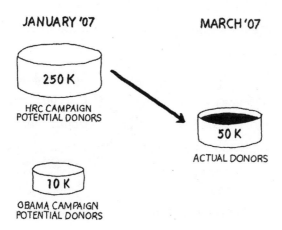

Meanwhile, the Obama For America (OFA) campaign started with at most ten thousand names, cobbled together in Excel spreadsheets. Clinton had a twenty-five-to-one advantage.

If we had used their approach, even managing the same stellar conversion rate, we would have ended up with only two thousand donors.

Instead, our campaign reported one hundred thousand donors at the end of March. So what happened? The Clinton campaign was hunting. Hunting very well, but hunting. They were happy to get a subset. It was division.

Our campaign could not afford to get a subset of such a small number. So we farmed. We multiplied. And that added up to not only more donors but more overall money to the primary election campaign: $19 million for Obama and $16 million for Clinton.

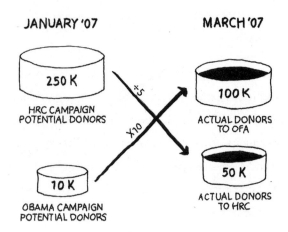

I encouraged the volunteers at the seminar to go back home and try something different. Don't try to win an argument, no matter how justified, no matter how compelling. Instead, sit everyone in a circle and ask each person to share a fear and a hope for this country. Bring a notepad and write it all down. Once everyone has had a chance to express themselves, they will often come up to you and thank you for the dialogue. Technically, you haven't had a dialogue because you haven't said much, but it feels that way. Then ask them to please do the same with other groups of their friends and neighbors.

That's what Obama was doing every day. That's what he was doing in that cornfield in Iowa. He knew the math: the fruitful friction of special relationships multiplies; the frustrating friction from arguing divides.

## THE CONSTELLATION BLOOMS

In fact, Obama had been to cornfields all over Iowa—and diners, living rooms, and factories. The campaign believed that to have any shot at beating Clinton, he had to surprise people in the Iowa caucus. Iowa was a place where Obama's multiplication might stand a chance against Clinton's support among party insiders. When caucus day finally arrived, I was there too.

For those not so versed in the mechanics of presidential elections (most happy people), the Iowa caucus kicks off the Democratic and Republican primary elections. I was assigned by our campaign to serve as a "caucus observer" at a school in northern Des Moines. My role was clear: when the caucus was done, report how it went via email, or if anything went amiss, send an urgent email so the campaign could decide whether or not to send in an elections lawyer.

Caucusing is kind of like group voting out in the open. Essentially, voters from a particular precinct gather in one big room. Everyone goes and stands under a sign with the name of their preferred candidate. You count the number of people in the room, and any candidate with more than 15 percent of the total is called "viable." Then there's a second round for people whose candidates didn't get enough votes to choose from the remaining, viable candidates. Each caucus site is worth a number of points (ours was five), and the viable candidates split those proportionally.

People like me had been sent all over the state because the race looked very close and we had to make sure we racked up every possible point. Iowa Democratic officials, including the governor, had virtually all endorsed Clinton, so the Obama campaign was nervous about possible interference.

I showed up with lots of time to spare and chatted with some other early arrivals. Seven women in their sixties who were all wearing Hillary for President T-shirts told me that they had been coming to this site since 1976 to caucus together. The candidate they endorsed had never lost the precinct. Two of their crew were delayed by a snowy night but would be arriving soon.

Then, abruptly, another woman with the clarity of a seventh-grade science teacher let us know she would be running the caucus. As 7:00 p.m. approached, she got everyone ready. Then caucus-goers were told to head to their respective corners, which had names on signs attached to the walls: Bill Richardson, John Edwards, Barack Obama, and Hillary Clinton, etc.

It was shocking. There were only eight in the Clinton corner—the seven women I had met plus one man. There were five people each in the corners for Richardson and Edwards. And in the Obama corner: sixty-four people. Brown, white, black—all ages. Someone in the Clinton corner asked in a stage whisper, "Who are these people?" This was great news for our campaign. Not only had we won, but we would get all five points. Not even Clinton had met the 15 percent threshold for viability. She had missed it by one person. I began to prepare my email to HQ with the good news.

Then, with a loud *ka-chunk*, a rear fire door opened, and two women walked in. The leaders stopped. It turned out these were the two missing members of the T-shirted team caucusing for Clinton. I wanted to jump up and say, "Wait, it's past seven. That's against the rules!" but, as an official campaign observer, I wasn't allowed to speak. I changed the subject heading of my email to "urgent: problem" just in case.

The caucus leader hushed everyone and spoke: "The rules are clear—only people in the room at seven p.m. are allowed. . . ." Whew. But she continued, "But there is also a rule . . . Well, I don't know if it's a rule, but it's a tradition here . . ." Uh-oh. ". . . that if we take a vote in the room, we can decide to amend the rules and let them in."

Okay, no problem. We had seventy-two of the ninety votes. The Obama corner talked among themselves and informally picked a leader, and she reported the consensus of the group.

"We all agree. Their votes should count," she declared.

What?! The hastily appointed leader, who saw my bewilderment, walked over and explained the group's decision to me. "This whole campaign is so everybody can be heard. Everybody respected, everyone included. Everybody means everybody."

The two late arrivals headed to the Clinton corner. Then the people in the nonviable Richardson and Edwards corners had to pick new candidates. All ten of them joined the Obama corner. They felt included too and had just seen it practiced and not just preached. Obama got four points. Clinton got one. I got a big lesson.

In fact, it was a deeper version of the lesson I had been trying to teach to fellow fundraisers in Chicago. Listening to others and sharing mutual hopes and fears as Obama had done with us in Louisville was indeed effective, but it was not a tactic. It was not part of a strategy to multiply in order to win. That would have been the Pyramid mindset. Instead, listening and sharing and being open *was* the campaign. It was both the means and the end. A listening campaign for a listening government. The "how" was the "what."

An entire year before caucus night, field offices for Obama began to crop up around the state. The leaders of field organizing, Steve Hildebrand and Paul Tewes, had put up a makeshift poster that was a reminder to all in the office of what we were doing and how we were doing it: RESPECT, EMPOWER, INCLUDE. It didn't come from Obama HQ in Chicago, but it spread around the state and eventually to every field office around the country. "Yes We Can" later became the official campaign slogan, but it was *respect, empower, include* that set the pattern and tone of the campaign, from which flowed bloom loops, interdependence, and the campaign Constellation.

This multiplication was enough to win the Iowa caucus, astonishing longtime political observers. It also posed unforeseen challenges to organizers. They'd never had so many people who wanted to be involved. Buffy Wicks and Jeremy Bird, the campaign point people in two pivotal states, California (because it held by far the largest number of delegates) and South Carolina (because the primary there was just a matter of weeks after Iowa), got on the phone to talk about how to make this surge of volunteer enthusiasm a blessing and not a curse.

They agreed to try a radical solution. For those who didn't skip the intro to this book, Buffy and Jeremy were the two un-named Obama staffers we met there.

Simplistically, the usual job of a campaign is to encourage its voters to turn out on Election Day and, cynical though it may be, to encourage everyone else not to. A campaign's "voter file," the list it has compiled of possible voters, where they live, and how likely they are to support its candidate (on a scale of one to five), is usually guarded like Fort Knox because otherwise it will find its way to the competition. The radical solution Buffy and Jeremy posed to Chicago HQ was to open up Fort Knox. Let committed volunteers have access to the voter file and take over many of the organizing duties themselves with some basic training.

The campaign leadership initially said no, fearing that there might be plants from other campaigns (spies, if you will) among the Obama volunteers. Buffy and Jeremy responded that they certainly couldn't guarantee there *wouldn't* be any spies, but they knew that most of the people definitely were *not* spies and their energy would be worth the risk of any potential data theft. And if they didn't open up the campaign, they would have to turn volunteers away. They had to relinquish some of their power in order to unleash the power of the group.

The campaign leaders agreed. Buffy and Jeremy contacted the firm that managed the online voter file to tell them to brace for an increase in traffic because it wouldn't be just a handful of paid staff accessing it but rather hundreds or maybe even thousands of volunteers. The people at the firm had seen so many campaign cycles they were at once condescending and reassuring: we got this. The day they opened the file, volunteers overwhelmed their servers with traffic and shut them down for a day. Oops. That firm learned a lesson too.

Buffy, Jeremy, and others soon put in some general protocols to maximize the energy. They would hire one paid organizer who would in turn recruit six or so "super volunteers"—people usually over sixty-five or under twenty-five who committed many hours a week. Every super volunteer would find ten regular volunteers who were each responsible for trying to get a certain number of likely voters to the polls.

When the campaign first went into a state, each paid organizer (the circle in the middle in the image on the next page) and their super volunteers would have a big section of a city (called "turf"). A true sign of their success was not expanding their turf, but the opposite. If you did a good job, your turf would shrink as more volunteers joined, your knowledge would deepen, and your relationships would grow. By the end, success looked like having turf of only, say, one city block.

It's called the snowflake model. By the day of the general election between Obama and Republican John McCain, it was at work in all fifty states.

It looked like this:

The Snowflake Model

On Election Day, a campaign's effort is no longer about persuading voters. It's about making sure the people who said they would support you actually vote. This is the big test of your volunteer network, as those volunteers have to fan out to make sure voters go to the polls. In the introduction of this book, I described the term *flake rate*, which is the percentage of pre-committed volunteers who flake out and don't show up. A really bad flake rate is 80 percent, where eight in ten don't show, and a really good one could be as low as 30 percent. To be safe, you plan on 50 percent. In one key battleground state that day, the flake rate for the Obama volunteers was *negative 50 percent*:

for every ten people who committed, fifteen showed up. It was new mathematical territory. You might call it the snowflake rate.

Think back to the two photos at the beginning of the chapter. When I looked out at those two million people on that cold January Inauguration Day from the bleachers behind that lectern, I didn't see a crowd. Or just individuals. I saw the group of twelve people from the cornfield in Iowa and imagined the twelve more that they respected, empowered, and included after Obama had moved along to the next town. And so on throughout Iowa, South Carolina, California, and Kentucky—the whole country. I saw individuals discovering themselves with and through small groups of others in pursuit of freedom together—giving away power and thereby creating more.

## THE SNOWFLAKE TEST

Barack Obama didn't grow the snowflake. The snowflake grew. The snowflake grew with the energy of *respect, empower, include* so that it could unleash more energy in a virtuous cycle for energy growth and energy capture. And it turns out this kind of self-repeating growth is common in nature.

We all know trees branch out and the branches and stalks get thinner as they spread. The whole tree is the result of a simple branching pattern repeating over and over. People have

been interested in this type of growth for a long time—above is a sketch by Leonardo da Vinci.

He shows a tree with a simple Y pattern repeated. People who study these repeating patterns call them "self-similar." And nature has all kinds of examples of things that grow with this self-similar branching quality.

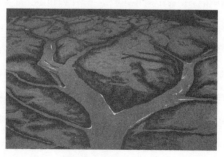

Like river deltas . . .

... broccoli ...

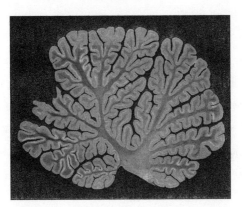

... and neurons in the brain.

These self-similar patterns are called fractals. Snowflakes—the real things—are also fractals. If you look at a snowflake under a microscope, you see it is made of tiny snowflakes. One of the reasons this kind of fractal growth is so successful—in trees, for instance—is that it can create something incredibly complex without a complex "master plan." Instead, it begins with a successful pattern (called a "seed pattern" in fractal speak) and repeats it. Trees use energy to create Y branches capable of capturing even greater energy from sunlight by covering more space and creating more surface area.

Constellations grow the same way. Obama's personal seed pattern and tone might be described as something like "listening to link up"—seeking to link others' hopes and fears to his own in a bond of interdependence that inspires the listener to also go out and listen to link (and so on). It was something he modeled in actions, words, and even small mannerisms. The campaign articulated it as *respect, empower, include.*

Once we understand self-similarity, it's easy to test ourselves along the way to see how true we are being to the pattern we preach. Let's call it the snowflake test. It asks a single, simple question: Is the pattern the same at any place and at any scale? Put another way, does the small pattern you just expressed or just observed look like the big thing you would want if you repeated it and repeated it? Are we shouting for calm? Throwing rocks for peace? Fighting for healing?

## DEATH AND LIFE

Close readers of this book will remember from chapter 3 that Mary Parker Follett had come to believe so much in the power of giving away power that she would die for it. That might have seemed eccentric or dramatic, but it would have made perfect sense to Jane Jacobs. Jacobs was born a generation later but shared Follett's penetrating clarity about the Pyramid and Constellation mindsets and the stakes of the struggle between the two. She is, for us, the great defender of the Constellation who, in her lifetime, which spanned decades of Pyramid dominance in our culture from the Great Depression through the Cold War, never wavered in her insistence that we must let go of power in order to let it grow.

Jacobs was a middle-class kid born in the middle of World War I in Scranton, Pennsylvania, who escaped to New York City as soon as she could after graduating from high school. She got her first job as a stenographer, where she honed an uncanny power of observation that first made her a good reporter and then a public thinker and writer who always defied labels, although she was often given them (her *New York Times* obituary headline combined two popular labels by calling her an "urban activist" when she died at age eighty-nine). Her power came from an ability to see the full scope of life as it is actually lived—not as it is feared or wished to be.

She first gained some fame in the 1950s for standing up to "power broker" Robert Moses in New York City and stopping his bulldozers from cutting a freeway system through Greenwich Village and Little Italy in the name of what he and his fellow progressive reformers called "slum clearance." She followed that with a bestselling book a few years later, *The Death and Life of Great American Cities,* which challenged the entire field of urban planning. Pop history tells us she fought Moses to save beautiful building facades and history and "urban fabric." Not at all. She was preserving life—groups of people in Constellations that energized an entire economy.

Jacobs saw Constellations all over, especially in thriving cities, with busy and shifting groups of neighbors and shopkeepers and industries making up their own seed pattern of competition and cooperation and co-creation. Like snowflakes, great cities to Jacobs were made up of great neighborhoods, and neighborhoods, in turn, of great blocks. She saw beautiful order in this complexity of life at any scale, while the Pyramid mindset, by contrast, saw chaos. The Pyramid imposed its own idea of order in the form of "superblocks" and big housing projects, which Jacobs saw as nothing less than killing life. Such plans failed the snowflake fractal test. Worst of all, they were being executed under the pretense of progress.

She tried to make her point stick by reminding us of how nature works. Think of a rainforest compared with a desert. Each gets the same amount of energy from the sun, but what they do with it is practically opposite. A rainforest recirculates and recombines the energy through many layers, from the canopy to the ground and beneath into the soil and root systems. A desert, on the other hand, takes that same amount of energy and absorbs only a small amount as heat and reflects almost all of it back up, unused and uncirculated.

The two keys for keeping all that energy in rainforests are branching and connecting. Plants literally branch, and animals figuratively do it with reproduction and species variation, and then it all interacts. There's cooperation. There's competition. There's co-creation. That's life.

Jacobs didn't accuse Robert Moses of trying to turn New York into a proverbial desert, but something close to that. She felt that when Moses and his ilk imposed "master plans" on a city—with separate designated zones for commerce, for sleeping, for industry, and so on—it left no possibility for branching and recirculating among and between things. While the simple order of a master plan might look pretty on an overhead slide projection, it led inevitably to what she called "plantation towns," a not-so-subtle indictment of the top-down power brokers and their systematic disempowerment of so many.

Dee Hock had the word *educe*; Jacobs had *ramify*. It's the root of *ramification*, as in consequences. But *ramify* alone means to branch or differentiate. It is an active verb. She felt that the branching is where energy finds new opportunity—branching out a new brand or product line, branching into a new location. It's these small, repetitive evolutions that make a profound impact over time. The more dynamic the environment—the more people you have with this mindset—the more energy will be created. And energy, which is just power repeatedly given away and returned, is the coin of the realm.

Jacobs kept writing books and kept showing up as an activist to prevent bulldozers from destroying life and paving the way for death. Toward the end of her life she was asked if she thought her greatest contribution was standing up to the bulldozers. "No," she said. Not at all. She did that only because they wouldn't stop trying to bulldoze things that grow. She thought her most important insight wasn't about preventing death so much as discovering patterns of life and how those patterns make successful things (cities, companies, economies, whatever) grow. She summed it up as her discovering "the fractal" in the realm of human affairs.

She taught us to look for heat. "To seek 'causes' of poverty . . . is to enter an intellectual dead end," she wrote, "because poverty has no causes. Only prosperity has causes." Heat has causes, but cold is just what's left when those processes are gone. That's why scientists study heat (thermodynamics) and there's no such field for the study of cold. "Just so, the great cold of poverty and economic stagnation is merely the absence of economic development. It can be overcome only if the relevant economic processes are in motion." Only with Constellations.

But if Jacobs was right, how could so many be so wrong? Why is it that, then and now, we look at life in all its diversity, complexity, and motion and choose a mindset that can only see it all as chaos? Talk about exhausting. Why? Because as we admitted at the outset of this book, we'll do almost anything to avoid what Jacobs viewed as a fundamental, inextricable, and inescapable aspect of growth: uncertainty. Remember, in life, we don't grow things. We have to let things grow. There's just no getting around it. Growth and uncertainty come as a package deal.

That's okay, though. More than okay. Uncertainty is never randomness, if we know how to use it. Uncertainty is potential energy like heat from the sun. Uncertainty is what makes the whole system work—we don't know what new branching will happen and which branches will grow and which will wither and which will connect with other branches. Jimmy Wales and Dee Hock used uncertainty to make rainforests, so to speak, and that's what all Constellation leaders do. They create the ecosystem for the use and reuse of energy at any scale. At the heart of this is Follett's prescription for the group process— bringing our whole selves, with our hurts and hopes (where the energy lives), and turning that into something productive that others can use and reuse and so on and so on.

For Jane Jacobs, and for Follett and Thomson and all the heroes we've met in this book, the Constellation is not an alternative model to be deployed in certain circumstances. The *Pyramid* is the alternative model—and it can be deadly dangerous. The Pyramid mindset—planning away uncertainty, extracting power from individuals for the purposes of simplification and single-mindedness, prizing stability above all else—can save us in an emergency, but it is also the mindset that leads to authoritarianism, patriarchy, and slavery. The Constellation, on the other hand, is not a "model" at all. It's nature's playbook. It's life itself.

# 6

## DAYLIGHT BETWEEN US

THE COMPANY I JOINED out of college in 1993 as the fourth employee was nobody's idea of sexy. It was something new, an "internet company," which I had to explain to my mother and my roommates alike. Our company's bet was that people were all going to have to figure out this computer stuff, so we wanted to create the computer magazine experience on cable TV, as well as on this new internet thing.

To give you a flavor of just how rudimentary this was, we sold VHS tapes for $19.99 that explained how to use the internet. We called ourselves CNET: The Computer Network. It would be a "network" in the TV sense and also a network in the sense of a collection of people all linked together. We didn't know what that would mean exactly, but it sounded big and bold at a time when we were small and bold.

Quietly, unglamorous publications like *PC Magazine*, *Computer Shopper*, and *Macworld* were gaining huge numbers of subscribers and advertisers. Soon they outsold the top three business magazines three to one. I must have regurgitated that factoid a thousand times. It was the pitch our co-founders made to each venture capital firm that turned us down, and the one I would repeat in lower-stakes encounters, like trying to get credit approval for a copy machine in one of my first jobs as "director of innovation."

Despite the broad title, my main project was to build an online service that helped people find "shareware"—this was mostly homemade software built for the fun of it, games like *Doom* and *Duke Nukem*, or fixes for common PC problems. People had been sharing this stuff for free or a suggested donation and storing it wherever they could—on servers hosted by universities, municipalities, or corporations around the world.

A civil engineer working in Slovenia knew that this global network of downloadable software was a great resource, but it was completely hidden to new users of the World Wide Web. So he developed a simple and searchable portal of sorts to make finding the stuff a little less baffling. He was happy to sell it to us so we could build it out properly. We spruced it up and relaunched it as shareware.com.

As the weeks went on, visits to our main site (cnet.com) grew nicely, but shareware.com took off. Traffic doubled daily. Shareware publishers came to us asking us to host their files. We didn't host, so we pointed them to the global network of servers. Our main competitor, Ziff Davis, which published *PC Magazine* and many others, took a different approach that emphasized quality over quantity. It hosted the downloads directly on its own server, offered access only to members, and bragged about expert curation of the shareware it did offer. But users voted with their clicks and came to us.

We realized we should find more ways to let people participate, so we allowed nonexpert visitors to voice their opinions on our product review pages. This was new at the time and something our competitors thought was crazy. Our thinking was that unlike our writers and editors, readers actually owned the ThinkPads and could tell us if the battery really did last on a flight from NYC to San Francisco as advertised. Even as the community grew, skeptics within the company and outside kept doubting it would last. "What do these users *get* in return?" Other than the opportunity to share what they knew and help each other out, they sometimes got a T-shirt.

# REVENGE OF THE PYRAMID

Now, at this point in the book, it's not so mysterious to us what was going on at CNET—a Constellation was forming. It had formed because of that original spirit of the internet—that seed pattern set by Vint Cerf and Bob Kahn—and because we had not inserted ourselves as gatekeepers. Instead we had set the conditions for special relationships, bloom loops, and branching. I was fascinated by what was happening and I could see the magic it was bringing, even if I couldn't exactly explain how or why at the time.

By 1998 the dot-com frenzy was bubbling but not yet bursting. We announced that we were going to spend $100 million on a marketing campaign. We had gone public two years before and had a big "war chest," as our bankers called it. I had wondered earlier why exactly we needed to spend that much. When I asked the CEO, he said, "Because we can and because it's a big number and people will report on it—this is a 'go big or go home' moment."

We hired a major outside firm to help us with the marketing message. After joyless brainstorming sessions in windowless conference rooms, the ad agency suggested a new tagline. We sponsored *Monday Night Football* that year. The tagline would be repeated there and on buses and billboards all over New York City and San Francisco.

Here is the poster version from our conference room at the office:

We really did that.

It was the exact opposite of everything we had learned. It had been the people who were passionate about shareware as a hobby, people who cared about laptop battery life, who had put us on the map. They were "friends" and very much not paid experts. But in this ad campaign, we positioned ourselves at the top. We were saying, "Come get smart from us," instead of saying, "This is a place where people like you can get together and help each other." Worse still, we started believing it.

We accepted the conventional wisdom that we were now in a winner-take-all fight for total dominance of our "space," and we dropped a big Pyramid on our blooming Constellation. Spending our war chest meant that the focus was no longer on serving customers. The focus was now on winning. And these were very clearly two different things. And win we did. CNET stock took off and we soon had three thousand employees around the globe.

Around this time I got married, and Brooke and I decided to move to her hometown of Louisville. I kept working for CNET but gave up my managerial responsibilities and assumed the solo job of chief strategy officer. I got invited to Harvard Business School to respond to a case study two professors had just published about all that CNET had done right in taking our marketing budget from $1 million to $100 million. The study's official name was "CNET 2000: Harvard Business School Case #800-284." There were no hard questions. The students mostly wanted to know how to replicate our success or join our company.

That was February 2000, just one month before the dot-com bubble burst and our stock price dropped from an all-time high of eighty dollars to a low of eighty cents. We forged a desperate merger with our archrival just to survive. Eventually, CNET would get back on its feet and sell to CBS. The case study has since been, in the lingo of HBS, "retired."

# REVENGE OF THE PYRAMID—PART 2

It was not until the Obama campaign, as we saw in the previous chapter, that I would get up close and personal and involved with the magic of the Constellation mindset. On Election Day 2008, with our negative flake rate, I didn't have a worry in the world that we might replicate the CNET mistake and let our Pyramid mindsets return. After all, there were now so many people all over the country who had become part of it.

Just a few days after the inauguration, I wasn't so sure.

On election night, the weight of the office had visibly occupied Obama's body. The financial crisis was at its height. Troop levels in Iraq were at their height. In Afghanistan, they were growing again. The litany of threats and the office's sheer complexity all seemed to demand a more commanding leadership style. Meanwhile, Republicans, by their own admission, had agreed to a plan to deny President Obama any wins on any issue—even those they ideologically supported. They felt Obamaism was the biggest threat of all.

Obama was about to take the unconventional step of going to Capitol Hill to talk with House Republicans, who were then in the minority, about the stimulus proposal to address the economic crisis. Eric Cantor from the Republican leadership team had given him a white paper that outlined his party's approach.

Obama had told him it was a reasonable place to begin discussion. Cantor said no—they weren't going to negotiate.

They wanted it all. They were essentially trying to surround Obama's Constellation with a Pyramid blockade. It was clear that fruitful friction with them was not possible.

*Respect, empower, include* had hit a partisan impasse, yet the massive network of volunteers the mantra had helped build still surged with the energy of millions. The official name of the campaign had been Obama for America, which was always shortened to OFA. Now that the campaign was over, a clever renaming allowed us to keep the acronym, and hopefully the energy too, by calling it Organizing for Action.

This network was now going to be wielded as a weapon to win important legislative battles yet to come. No one thought this was a bad idea. In fact, we all considered it a no-brainer. Yet this no-brainer ended up killing the magic at the heart of the Constellation. What happened?

We unwittingly did what so many Constellations before and since have done. We took the Pyramid mindset's bait. To put a point on it, and to our cheers, Obama told the Republicans, "Elections have consequences. . . . I won."

Here's the thing: elections have consequences for the winner too, and not all of them are good. Not only does a candidate win, but winning-and-losing also wins. The Pyramid mindset wins. The Washington establishment and the media know only this battle mode. Not surprisingly, the "elections have consequences" quip became famous again less than two years later: the Republicans hurled it back when they won control of the House in the midterm elections.

## COMMITTING TO A NEW PATTERN AND TONE

This time, unlike at CNET, I was determined not to lose the way of seeing, thinking, and behaving that I was starting to embody, even if I still couldn't fully articulate it. I wanted to continue Obama's pattern and tone, but I also knew that mine would be a little different. Obama is a singular talent who possesses skills I'd never be able to replicate, but I had my own talents and worldview that I wanted to bring to bear. President Obama asked me to be his ambassador to Sweden and I committed myself to keeping the Pyramid mindset at bay.

I knew it would be hard. Then my first few weeks in the State Department orbit confirmed just to what degree. Of course we think of bureaucracy when we think of federal agencies, but the State Department has always had a reputation of being more open and creative than its much bigger pentagonal sibling across the river. The Defense Department, with its life-and-death mandate, gets many times more attention and money, but State was supposed to be home to practitioners of "statecraft"—the daily art of promoting amity and preventing conflict. State was a distributed network with embassies—little plots of America—spread all over the world.

The State Department hosts a two-week orientation for new ambassadors called "Charm School." That might conjure images of lessons in persuasion or maybe how to hold one's teacup with a prince, but it turned out to be neither. Everyone who comes from outside the US Foreign Service (roughly 30 percent of ambassadors) is given a guide to help them through the process. Mine was Carl, and when I asked him what I could expect from these two weeks, he leveled with me: "I'll tell you the truth. It's mostly death by PowerPoint."

He was right. It was deck after deck of PowerPoint introductions to the State Department's org charts and infinite acronyms. To offer you a taste, as one presenter tried to bring yet another org chart to life with animated arrows that appeared between the acronym-crammed boxes, he augmented the slide with this commentary:

> All of you are in EUR, so if you have issues, you can ask your PDAS to consult with M about budgets, but make sure to go through IX/IO, as they are the gatekeepers, unless of course R has extra money (they often do), but money here isn't fungible, so if you want to complain you can get in line with H.

(For those interested, here's an English translation: "You are in the European division, so if you want to find extra money for a program, you need the help of the principal deputy assistant secretary of state for Europe, and they can try to get the money the normal way or, if that fails, from the Public Diplomacy Bureau, but that probably won't work because Congress controls the budget." Or simpler still: "Don't ask for more money.")

Sadly, Charm School was an accurate reflection of the state of State. On the last day, Carl supplemented his dim view of the orientation with a broader warning about the culture of the State Department. He told me a story about Colin Powell, then a few weeks into his job as George W. Bush's secretary of state, having previously served many distinguished years over at the Department of Defense.

Secretary Powell and his team of career foreign service officers sat around a table in the formal conference room on the seventh floor of the Main State Building. It was known as the "power floor," where the senior-most people worked. With its wood-paneled walls, it looked nothing like the rest of the building, which had the charm of a run-down hospital complete with industrial-width hallways and fluorescent lights.

He looked around at his team and, the story goes, said something like, "I don't think everyone here understands the secret to how this town works. It's all about what you as a department or agency have that no one else does." Then he asked, "What do you think the Navy has that no one else has?"

Someone finally guessed, "Ships?"

"Not ships. Coast Guard has ships. The answer is aircraft

carriers—our huge, floating platforms to project power. That's the Navy's unique thing. How about the Air Force?"

Somebody meekly suggested planes. "Not planes. Marines have planes, Army has planes. The Air Force has missiles. The really big ones out west."

"Now," he asked them, "what's our special thing here at State?"

At this point, one participant finally thought he had the answer and said with confidence not yet expressed by the others, "This place. Main State, the Harry S. Truman Building."

"Nope. That's not it. Everyone has a building. Some have five sides, others have four. We all have buildings here in the capital. No, what we have here at State is two-hundred-twenty-some-odd platforms for diplomatic engagement spread throughout the world. They are called embassies. But walking around this building you would never even know they exist."

Powell could see what those who had worked there for longer had forgotten to see. His team looked up to the top of Pyramid power—the White House, for those in Washington. They imagined their relative importance and saw scarcity. Powell looked the other way, out at a Constellation, and saw abundance.

## A TEST PATTERN

The Pyramid mindset of State during Charm School distressed me. When it was over, it was time to visit the White House to be officially sent off as President Obama's ambassador. I wasn't sure exactly what I'd find there.

The "Oval," so often photographed and re-created for films and shows like *The West Wing*, looked exactly as I thought it would. But what was genuinely surprising was how the whole place sounded and felt—how hushed the White House was and how restrained by office clothes and careful manners the young staffers were. They had been dynamos of pure energy during the campaign. Now the air surrounding them was heavy and dutiful.

The president, on the other hand, was relaxed, warm, and open in his elliptical surroundings. After the pleasantries and formalities, I had only one real question for him. So, when I took my seat at the edge of the sofa and he took his seat in the chair to my right, I jumped straight in.

"Mr. President, do you have any advice for a first-time diplomat?"

He sat back and clasped his hands around his knee and stared up at the chandelier for a bit longer than I'd expected. Then he looked at me and said, "Well, Matthew, listen."

And I thought to myself as a beat passed, "Yes, sir, of course I'll listen to you. . . . That's why I asked. . . ." I sat there with my little black notebook opened to the first page and my pen out, poised to write down pearls of wisdom. But another beat passed and then another. And it took me an awkwardly long time to realize that he wasn't saying, "Prepare to listen to all

my great forthcoming advice." His advice for a first-time diplomat was simply "Listen."

I carried the president's guidance with me to Stockholm
alongside a lesson from my father-in-law, offered years before.
He made whiskey. He was a distiller from Kentucky, as well as
a CEO, painter, philanthropist, and more. He was full of wisdom. He explained to me that there are three steps required to
make whiskey. Those three steps were a metaphor for making
good things of all kinds.

The first is fermentation. You need natural ingredients, including a tiny thing that's practically invisible: yeast. That's the
catalyst that gets the water and grains all bubbling up. And this
bubbling can happen only if you have the right environment—
too hot or too cold and it won't work. If you stop at this stage,
you have beer (but not the kind you'd want to drink).

The second step is distillation. Refining down to just the
essentials. But if you stop here, you get what is essentially vodka.
Nothing wrong with vodka, he said, but you can make vodka
in an afternoon.

The third step? I thought I knew this: ageing. Nope. Not
quite. Time is part of it, he explained, but it is time in a barrel.
The technical term is *maturation*. And the key is that it is time
in a barrel getting warmer and getting cooler with the seasons,
over and over. Time to expand and contract—pulling color and
character and complexity out of the barrel and into the whiskey.

The lesson helped me then and ever since as a way to think

about agreement and disagreement, gratitude and resentment, competition and cooperation. *Listen* and *whiskey* were my watchwords as I began as a diplomat. I think Follett would have endorsed them because listening implies needing others and whiskey implies change by way of a deliberate process.

# FIRST-TIME DIPLOMAT

The external appearance and the internal feeling of the US Embassy in Stockholm is the product of two big factors: the Cold War and 9/11. It feels to Swedes like something of a midcentury-style fortress on a hill ornamented with telecom doodads that look like they're meant for espionage. The building represented what Swedes mistrusted about the United States.

I made it a priority to change our cloistered reputation to foster a Swedish-American Constellation. After heavy back-and-forth with our wonderful and sometimes (understandably) skeptical embassy staff, we rolled out what we called the US Embassy Road Show. I welcomed staff who wanted to raise their hands and get involved, and I also assured them it was totally okay to stay back at the embassy and do that important work there. It wasn't an in-or-out test.

Coming from Louisville, I knew that smaller cities really appreciate visitors, so I decided we would first visit places that usually don't get the love and attention they deserve. There were many cities to choose from—Sweden is the geographical size of California with the population of Chicago—but we decided on Umeå, one of the faster-growing cities up north and a university town.

In the early morning, right in the town center, we unrolled the red awning of our classic Airstream Bambi trailer, hooked up to our Chevy Avalanche FlexFuel pickup truck. Then we set up some tables to cook an American pancake breakfast. The plan was for me to make pancakes outside for curious passersby.

We had tested the new electric griddles in Stockholm to make sure they would perform as hoped. It was probably ten degrees Celsius when we tested them, but now it was minus seven. As a TV crew interviewed me, my colleague from the press office caught my eye to signal that I should stop rubbing my hands together. Too late. The interviewer noticed, and evening news viewers were treated to a visual joke about politicians and shaking hands.

While I served barely cooked pancakes, other team members set up our "embassy in a box," where people could perform basic embassy business like obtaining certain visas. It was essentially a pop-up consulate along with some fun Americana and interactive stuff. We made friends and stayed in touch. We hit cities like Linköping and Växjö. With a big American truck and Airstream trailer and a red carpet and an open door, we weren't earning points for subtlety. But that was the whole idea. We were opening ourselves up for more conversations.

I dutifully did the "big" important things involving our European alliances, troop levels, trade deals, terrorism, etc.—but I also wanted us to see these new "small" things, like the road show and other initiatives, as just as important. We were forming special relationships and setting a new pattern and tone.

It felt to me like things were just beginning to pick up steam and the whole embassy was starting to buy in when President Obama called to ask me to come back early from my posting to serve as his finance chair for his reelection campaign. He knew this campaign would be different and made a point to tell me that I didn't have to say yes. It was nice of him, and he meant it. But I felt like I did have to say yes. The person who had sent me on this mission to listen was now asking me to join another. If I stayed in Sweden nothing would change externally and, in fact, no one would even have to know about the offer, but something crucial would change internally for me. The role would instantly lose its connection to a purpose higher than my own, as Lynne Twist would say, and would just be a job I liked doing. We packed our bags.

## WORKING BACKWARD

If the 2008 Obama campaign was a wave to be surfed, the 2012 reelection felt more like swimming back out against the waves. A slog. If 2008 had been the good math of multiplication, 2012 was the crude math of adding small fractions on our side and subtracting them from our opponents. In short, the Constellation mindset was fully eclipsed by the Pyramid mindset.

This time we had a huge database of volunteers and supporters. We could win by getting a subset of them to show up again, to give again, and to bring some fraction of the excitement they had brought before. We would have to live with a flake rate. The field team—made famous by Buffy and Jeremy and all the folks who created the snowflake model—was now rebranded as Team 270, reminding us of the bare minimum number of electoral votes required to win. Getting any more wasn't necessary. Reaching everybody wasn't necessary. We just needed to work backward from that number to win. Anyone walking into the campaign HQ was greeted with a giant version of the famous sign from Iowa four years before with one telling addition: RESPECT, EMPOWER. INCLUDE. WIN.

In the early days of the Obama campaign in 2007, there was a man and a message and not much else. We had to ask for help from anywhere we could get it and from anybody who would give it. This forced us to practice the traits that made us so good at multiplying—listening, inclusion, humility. The campaign was about "we"—always "we" and not a forced "we."

During the reelection, one of the most shared social media memes was a photo of Obama in sunglasses with the text "Chill the f*** out, I got this." It's funny and it's also telling. In 2008 we got supporters "fired up"; in 2012 we told them to "chill out." 2008 was "yes we can"; 2012 was "I got this." This is an over-simplification to be sure, but it still contains some truth about the difference in pattern and tone. The campaign was the first to raise a billion dollars, and I was enormously relieved—rather than elated like in 2008—that Obama won reelection decisively.

He asked me to serve as an ambassador again—this time to the United Kingdom. It's considered a plum job, and it is, but I was mostly excited because I got to pick up where I'd left off in Sweden on making Constellations and refining a better pattern.

It was also not the easiest time to be there, which I relished. A British friend joked upon my arrival that my predecessor served during a royal wedding, the Queen's Diamond Jubilee (sixtieth anniversary as monarch), and the London Olympics. I, on the other hand, would have a vote by Scotland deciding whether it should leave the UK, a referendum on whether the UK should leave the European Union, and a presidential election back home during Obama's last, "lame duck" year.

## THE QUEEN AND THE COMEDIAN

The formal start of our posting was the ambassador's presentation of credentials to Her Majesty the Queen. Brooke and I had been briefed thoroughly on the whole thing: where to put my top hat, when to bow and curtsy, and who would signal what to do when. Once inside the palace, everything went exactly as we'd been told. Brooke and I had our "audience." Her Majesty had been briefed on my background in the internet and technology sector and asked me about that. I said something bland and obvious about how fast it was changing and how nearly all the tourists outside the palace always had at least one, and often more than one, tech device.

"Yes. And you know, I miss it," she said. "There have always been cameras of course . . . but they used to snap a picture and then put those down around their necks and wave or wave back. Now it's those rectangles covering their faces . . ." She lifted her white-gloved hand and held it in front of her eyes, simulating a smartphone, as she continued, "And they never put it down. I miss seeing their eyes."

A few days later, I mentioned to a trusted person that this comment had really stuck with me. (Unfortunately, a member of the press was within earshot and there's an unwritten rule that one should never speak to the press about private conversations with the Royals. The press was as gleeful about the mistake as Buckingham Palace was gracious about my apology.) Gaffe aside, what she said hit me in that moment and has stuck with me ever since. "I miss seeing their eyes." And this is the real point, which never would have occurred to me. We think of it as a one-way thing—the tourist snapping and the

Queen being snapped. But it isn't—or wasn't, at least for her. It was a connection. And she missed it.

As I sat with her words, they felt like a lament for our times—a perfect expression of our being so connectable yet feeling so disconnected. It fueled my efforts to push this other style of leading even as I learned on the fly. Just a few weeks later I stumbled upon another expression of this idea in a very different setting. I'd been seated at a dinner party next to British stand-up comedian Jimmy Carr. I was alternately laughing and cringing for the first half hour, then I caught my breath to ask him a question I had always wondered, never having met a comedian before. "If you're trying out ten brand-new jokes for a new stand-up routine, how many will get a laugh the first time?"

"You mean now or when I got started? Because after twenty years of practice I'm getting pretty good," he told me. "Right now? I'd say I'm up to as high as three out of ten."

That made me feel better about my own hits and misses, and I was about to dutifully turn to talk to the person on my right, but Jimmy wasn't done. And it was what he said next that really struck me. "You know, Matthew, jokes are funny things. I mean they are strange things," he said. "Think about it: If you play a song and no one likes it, it's still a song. If you write a play and everyone walks out, it's still a play. But if you tell a joke and no one laughs, it's just a sentence."

To me, that was profound. A joke isn't just the delivery of the words. It's the connection—a completed circuit. The comedian does his or her part; the audience does theirs. And together they create something new. It's no longer just you and me. It is us. Engaged. Otherwise, it's just a sentence. That's what the Queen had experienced.

As an imperfect practitioner of what I now call Constellation leadership, I found that this insight helped me better understand what I was learning and what I was trying to do—to create spaces, big and small, that passed the Jimmy Carr test. This charge of energetic connection is what makes special relationships, setting off bloom loops and setting the right pattern for interdependence.

## WE DO THIS TO OURSELVES

Soon after I got settled in at the embassy, I wanted to get a baseline of how the staff *felt* about things—not just what they thought. I conducted an informal exercise with the ten-person senior team. In the diplomatic world, the London team is known as one of America's superstar groups, composed of accomplished professionals who have served for decades in the foreign service. I warned them that this exercise would be a little different.

I asked them to draw a picture of what it felt like on a frustrating day working in foreign service at the State Department. (My wife has a master's in art therapy, and though I didn't use those words, that's really what this was.) They were, unsurprisingly, hesitant at first—"I'm not a good artist," and so on—but kindly went with it. I said they could draw themselves as stick figures and use shapes and arrows, or whatever worked for them.

Their pictures were different in many ways—for instance, some people drew themselves as big stick figures, others drew themselves tiny, and one drew just a circle with "*me*" inside. All ten doodles, however, were identical in one respect. Believe it or not, every person drew a big triangle somewhere on the page with themselves, in whatever form, at the bottom. One named the top of his triangle *DC*; another wrote *Main State* at the top. Then came the arrows. Some drew them raining down from above. Others used arrows to indicate their attempted ascent of the triangle while boulder-like objects of various sizes cascading down on them.

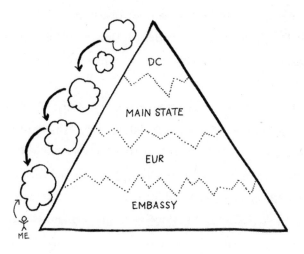

Then I made a plan to get everyone in the embassy to participate in a similar workshop—fifty people at a time. The idea wasn't wildly popular, but I loved what happened when people from different parts of the org chart sat together and were given the space and encouragement to think about the why, how, what, and who of their work life. I hadn't yet learned about Mary Parker Follett, but encouraging a mentality of integration and making things together was what I was reaching for.

At the beginning of each session, I asked each person to write down on an index card one word that described what frustrated them most about their job. Then on the other side of the card, they each wrote one word that best captured what inspired them most and gave them joy about working at the embassy. We collected the cards and used them to create a word cloud. Despite the question being totally open-ended, the answers were the same at all twenty workshops.

By far, the word most commonly written for frustration was *bureaucracy*. The most common for what inspired them: *community*.

I shared the findings with my deputy chief of mission, Liz. She nodded in her wise and reassuring way. "Ah, you see what's happening?"

I nodded in my "not really, but please go on" way.

"It's the same thing."

"What's the same?" I asked, still not getting it.

"It's us. We are the bureaucracy and we are the community. We do this to ourselves."

When the community instinct to engage and be hospitable and diplomatic is suppressed and turned inward, it becomes the anxious desire to defend one's turf. The result is bureaucratic Pyramids that hurl down the rocks my senior team doodled. It's an analog of Lynne Twist's rule about money. When community is inclusive and dynamic, it heals. When it's insular and stagnant, it "kills." Think death by PowerPoint.

The sessions turned out to be cathartic. They had the loosening effect I'd hoped they would. But the Pyramid mindset was constantly reasserting itself. Official meetings were diplomatic in name only. The most important people sat in the middle of their side, flanked by staff in order of seniority. The conference room table wasn't triangular, but it certainly felt very much like a hierarchical pyramid transposed to a table. The "principal"—the highest-ranking person—would have a list that they had worked on with their team and would guide the discussion.

Who and how many attended these meetings were subjects of tremendous interest and angst in the State Department. Weeks of haggling: Is it P(rincipal)+3 or P+5? Once it was locked in at, say, P+3, then the jockeying began about who the three staffers would be.

It was that familiar bad math. (P+3) + (P+3) equaled something less than eight and even less than two. The two principals had nothing resembling a normal conversation. They would read lines while being watched by their own side as much as by the other. I always brought my notepad but someone else was inevitably assigned to be the notetaker, usually the most junior person. The tone of voice and the body language were all wrong: each country sitting opposite the other like adversaries negotiating a surrender, no eye contact with your own team, just locking eyes with your "opposite number."

The embassy in London had a Protocol Office that managed the list of embassy contacts, especially for the ambassador, and served as greeters to events at Winfield House, the ambassador's residence, where my family lived. The pattern of behavior built up over decades was for the Protocol Office to be "gatekeepers" sorting out who should be seen with my family and me and who should be avoided. It was the up-down-in-out Pyramid instinct to keep the list small and exclusive. They were lovely people in the Protocol Office, but they had been encouraged over many years to filter people out.

Someone at some time told the members of the Protocol Office that this was the job. I think the idea was that if you create an atmosphere of exclusivity, then those who are allowed in will feel special. In reality, everyone ends up feeling like an impostor. And not only that: when we're made to feel like jerks, we're more likely to act like jerks too. It's a special transaction billed as a special relationship, and therefore it feels all the emptier. The magic of happy group dynamics, whether in person or virtual, is for everyone to feel powerful and vulnerable at the same time. Too often we were doing the opposite of this, and it just seemed toxic.

So we replaced that office with a new one called the Office of Network Engagement. By design it spelled the word ONE. As a culture in the embassy, and in the State Department more widely, we seemed to have such a joy for process and for policy and no corresponding joy for a third *P*: people. We knew, as diplomats, that people, not aircraft carriers, were our special advantage. Everyone said that. No one acted like that. Too many of us thought that human engagement was someone else's job. So the first act of ONE was to emphasize that even though we had forty-seven different branches of government representing nine cabinet-level offices within our building, we were *one* embassy with a common mission.

We also wanted to underscore the point that each person we engaged with outside the building was "one" in the sense of being an integrated, full person, just like each of us, and not merely a title on a business card. They had former jobs, they had partners and school ties, they had personal passions and hobbies and nonprofit boards they served on, they were members of diaspora communities from countries they cared about— all the stuff that we know makes up our full story but we so often factor out. We needed to start factoring all that *in* so we could make the most of the energy and wisdom that lay beyond our walls. Because the word *network* has been so dulled by overuse as a verb, adjective, and noun ("Go network at a networking event to build your network"), I took to thinking of ONE as an acronym for "only need everybody."

## 20,000 INDEX CARDS

Embassies have a way of tuning out vast numbers of people in the host country because they don't yet have a proper job or no longer have a certain job title. In essence, people under thirty and people over sixty-five. We wanted to see the UK as one country, to consider the many voices that comprise it as we expanded our network.

Around the time I was preparing for that first audience with Her Majesty at the beginning of my posting in the UK, the Pew Research Center released results of a global poll of young people. A survey of forty countries showed that attitudes about America had generally improved as President Obama began his second term, but there was one data point that disturbed us. Of all the forty nations surveyed, there was only one where young people had a lower regard for the United States than their parents—the UK. It seemed the Special Relationship was losing its special relationships over generations. The energy was flagging.

By then, I was alive to the importance of setting the proper pattern and tone and allergic to trying to do anything Pyramid-like or isolated. Most of the suggestions from early sessions with my team felt too much like that: We could give a lecture series on US foreign policy at universities. Or we could "fight for budget" to do "paid social media promotion" to "push out our policy." This all felt like wasting energy. I wouldn't want to be on the other side—being lectured to and having policy pushed at me. The idea of "solving" this problem with a big campaign of any kind felt to me like an irresponsible use of time, money, and effort.

The seed pattern of the 2008 campaign had come with me to Stockholm and had evolved with my style and my new role in diplomacy. I believed that if we were going to make a real difference, we needed to start in a cornfield, so to speak, or, in this case, a school. Our staff was used to arranging events where the ambassador would speak to the entire student body, but I was interested in a smaller group with more back-and-forth. We settled on a sixth form college (high school seniors, basically) in a not-fancy, not-struggling area of London.

The students were assembled when I arrived. I briefly introduced myself before asking them some questions. I wanted the students to know I was there to hear from them. They answered politely. And briefly. They were waiting for me to launch into my spiel like people wearing suits and ties are supposed to. It was awkward.

Luckily, I had prepared a trick for later in the conversation, borrowed from my sessions with my embassy team by way of my wife, Brooke. I figured I'd better not wait. I handed out index cards and State Department pencils and asked the students to draw a picture or write a word on each side of the card. On the first side, they wrote or drew what frustrated, confused, or concerned them about the United States. On the other side, what inspired them or gave them hope about the US.

This brought relief. They relished the opportunity to fill up the "frustrated" side and dived right in. They didn't seem to have much trouble with the "inspired" side either. Then I had them raise their hands and share what they'd written and drawn. As they spoke up, I repeated their answers and my colleague from the embassy wrote them on giant flip-chart paper we'd brought.

There was one issue that frustrated the students the most by far. It wasn't Syria or Iraq or surveillance or any foreign policy topic that had been in the news or that I had been quizzed on in my "murder boards" preparing for Senate confirmation. It was guns. Second and third on the list of frustrations, confusions, and concerns were racism and police brutality.

I started telling them about Kentucky and its hunting culture. They thought that sounded pretty ridiculous. I explained

I'm one of the ridiculous people who owns a shotgun for hunting, and I talked about what we wear. They laughed and judged. For kids from a country with no written constitution, they knew a lot about ours. We talked about the Second Amendment and the NRA. By the end, they were making fun of my American pronunciation of certain words and making fun of themselves, and in general it felt like I'd been allowed in—like they were letting me sit at their table in the cafeteria.

When it was done and I was heading back to the office, I had a very strong feeling that we were onto something. We did another and another. There was concern at the embassy that I was squandering my time and diverting from opportunities to go on TV or speak to larger crowds of influential people. After the fourth school, the young foreign service officer who had accompanied me said, "Sir, are we done now?" He could see my look of confusion. "They're all the same," he added. I tried to explain that these sessions weren't focus groups or good optics for a potential newspaper story. They were the work of diplomacy—the pattern and tone of organized listening that builds trust, respect, and understanding, one person at a time. We increased our pace to two per week and decided I wouldn't travel anywhere in the UK without fitting in a sixth form visit.

We developed a system where the students used clickers to answer questions. (For example: Have you visited the US? Click 1 for yes, 2 for no, and 3 for yes, but only Florida.) We watched their collective results on a screen in real time. That helped the quieter students get engaged. My favorite part of each workshop lasted only a split second. I would tell them the story about Obama's advice to me in the Oval Office to listen, then look at one student and say something like, "I'm here to listen to you, because, no pressure, you are the future leaders and decision makers of the United Kingdom." At 98 percent of the schools, the student would look behind and around like "Who, me?" And then they'd see their classmates looking at them and sit just a tiny bit taller and say with their eyes, "Yeah, okay, maybe me."

When I went to one of the "elite" schools, like Eton or Harrow, I would say that same line and look at one young person. But they didn't look behind or to the side or show any hint of "Who, me?" They just looked me right back in the eye as if to say, "Well spotted, sir."

It was interesting. At those selective schools, the students' pictures, words, and responses were generally the same as at any school. The only real difference was that "well spotted" moment, and I recognized it in a younger version of myself. It's the language and body language of entitlement, and it's deadly. It locks others out, and it locks you in. It's a pattern and tone that has no spreading power—in fact, it has the opposite of spreading power. It's like the necktie gifts to people who don't wear neckties. It is an energy killer within and without.

Word got around that we were doing these visits, and local

journalists began reporting on them. British elected officials called to ask what I was hearing. I ran into parents who said I'd visited their kids' schools and that it had meant something to the family. When we hit the hundred-school mark, *The New York Times* ran a story and included a copy of the word cloud that we updated after each visit, showing all the frustrations, confusions, and concerns.

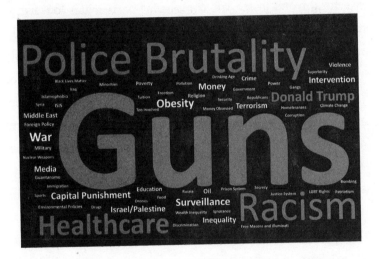

I got calls from the administration and other ambassadors about how they might replicate what we were doing. The British secretary for education even publicly declared that he was instituting a "listening" program at the center of his reform effort—explicitly patterned after our school visits.

# MY PATTERN AND TONE

With all this interest and momentum, the State Department tasked an embassy official with the job of "codifying" what we were doing. The talented young officer created a four-inch-thick binder with twenty tabs. I had a few meetings to get a sense of that effort. It was factual, accurate, well labeled, and easy for anyone to see the component parts—just like a dissected frog in science class. I steered clear of that exercise. To me, it felt like a very well-meaning, very effective way to kill whatever magic this pattern and tone had set.

However, it forced me to try to offer an alternative that would reflect this Constellation mindset approach. When faced with such Pyramid-style efforts, it is tempting to just walk away in frustration. However, it's a fatal mistake for Constellation mindset leaders to shy away from efforts to organize and codify because the Pyramid mindset assumes that its type of order (hierarchy) is order itself. All the Constellation mindset prophets and practitioners we've met thus far cared deeply about organizing, and about orienting the Constellation around a pattern and tone.

I decided it was time to do my best to articulate the pattern and tone I had been using. I called it "a.l.s.o." Here is the gist: to form special relationships, we can <u>ask</u> others about their hopes and fears, <u>link</u> them to our own, <u>serve</u> the relationship between us, and <u>open</u> ourselves up.

a.l.s.o. implies that there is always room for more—also your contribution and hers and his, also tomorrow and the next day, also our feelings and hopes and concerns. It was an attempt to break out of the Pyramid's isolated system of thinking and to promote energy creation and be watchful for energy destruction.

a.l.s.o. passed the Jimmy Carr test. It helped create an atmosphere for good "jokes" with the students instead of just sentences. a.l.s.o. passed the Jane Jacobs test too by allowing the discussion to grow in unexpected directions. It got me in the right place in the classrooms, but also in state rooms and Parliament and even at home. It still does. By the end of my tenure, I had been to two hundred schools and listened to and learned from twenty thousand British students. Members of my team had visited one hundred schools on their own and applied their own patterns and tones to the same goal.

The success of the school visits spawned a young professionals' group that organized with the embassy's support. We seeded it (so to speak) in a small city way outside London and asked some graduate students if they were interested, and four applied. The application was simple: just make a short smartphone video with one hope for the Special Relationship, one fear, and one image of what it means to them. Some on the team were skeptical about whether the group would make a splash. I didn't want it to; I wanted it to grow. And it did—to over two thousand by the end of my time.

When well-known Americans passed through London, as they did all the time, we would ask them if they wanted to talk with the group by phone or in person if we could find a space. No dignitary we asked ever said no. And those who said yes suggested it to their peers. No one flaked. They were as delighted to have the chance to hear from these future leaders as the young people were to hear from them.

Near the end of his presidency, Obama came to London for his last visit in office and held a town hall with our group, now called Young Leaders UK. The British had never heard of such a thing as a "town hall," but they were eager to be with the president. As soon as it began, it was clear that he loved it as much as they did. He took off his jacket and rolled up his sleeves. As the session went on, he talked less and listened more. Near the end, a young woman with a Welsh accent asked him, "Do you have any advice for a young person wanting to make a positive change in the world?"

He thought for a moment. Yes, he did. He said, "Be predisposed to see the power in other people."

There it was: that pattern and tone I had seen in the cornfield, still alive and well—and multiplying. Our young leaders group expanded fast after that. This was Obama at his best again. Asking for hopes and fears. Linking to his own. Serving and opening up.

# DAYLIGHT

Near the end of my time in the UK, Brooke and I were "guests of honor" at a dinner in London hosted by a retired British Army general with a group of distinguished and decorated British couples. The guest list tested my ability to remember that if someone is a lord *and* an admiral, in what order do you list the titles? (Admiral the Lord Doe or Admiral Sir John, for what it's worth.) We started with a toast to the Special Relationship at a fancy private club and then crossed the street to a crowded Italian restaurant and found our way to a long private table at the back. It had been a long day. I had flown home to London after spending the day in Edinburgh and Glasgow, Scotland, for meetings about the upcoming Scottish referendum as well as a high-energy workshop with sixth formers.

After the first course, I was expected to offer a "tour d'horizon" (a term I had learned earlier with a sigh). This meant that I should survey the world and its serious foreign policy topics, and give the US's perspective. This wasn't new. I even had a mnemonic device to keep them straight: let's look east and talk about the Russians trying to redraw the boundaries at the barrel of a gun; look south to Syria; look west to the proposed trade and investment deal between the US and the EU; look north to the melting polar ice cap. You get the idea. These were topics we picked apart in briefings every day—topics I'd been grilled on by State Department officials before my Senate testimony—answers I'd heard in meetings with the president and secretary of state, and issues journalists grilled me about.

But something wasn't right. As I sat with my back to a window, Brooke looked at me and I could make out the words she mouthed from across the table. "Are you okay?"

I wasn't okay. I felt light-headed. I subtly unbuttoned the top button of my shirt and loosened my tie just a fraction of an inch. That didn't work. I pardoned myself and edged by the other guests on my way to the bathroom. There was a small flight of stairs down into the main dining room. I paused and put my hand on the rail. And then . . . nearby diners were treated to the thud of my body hitting the carpet. I awoke several moments later on my back, my head resting in the arms of Simon, a member of my security detail. I was staring up at the ceiling. In the intervening seconds, I had projectile vomited and passed out. Or the other way around. I'm not sure.

Simon was smiling. But not because he was laughing at me. It was because I was smiling too. I felt strangely ecstatic. Because with that thud came a glorious insight—clear as the Iowa sky. I knew why I had passed out. It wasn't food poisoning—I was forced to undergo medical tests afterward and I knew they wouldn't find anything. It wasn't the company either. They could not have been lovelier or more supportive both before and after. It was me.

Something inside me decided I wasn't going to do it anymore. I knew that adopting the heavy voice that tries to convince yourself and others that you have it all figured out—that "often wrong but never in doubt" tone of voice that is meant to sound certain and win arguments but sounds more than a little controlling—is deadly.

Giving a tour d'horizon required pretending that I knew everything, that I would command from the top of a Pyramid. I'd learned to fake it and adopt the tone of the foreign policy establishment, in which a "muscular" culture of posturing rather than connecting too often dominates. But pretending is exhausting and corrosive. And I believe pretending is the opposite of what diplomacy demands.

Diplomats ought to live in the in-between—in the awkward seven times out of ten that the joke doesn't land. The task of a diplomat is to first learn how to become comfortable in that space and then to make others comfortable—to draw people out from behind their walls of entrenchment or entitlement into engagement. That's what turns frustrating friction into fruitful friction. And while Diplomacy with a capital $D$ is a job, the lowercase version is what we can all learn to do as we try to help Constellations grow.

Diplomats have a traditional stock reply at the ready whenever serious issues of potential disagreement among allies come up. When a diplomat is pressed on policy differences between countries, their reflexive response—a set piece—is to say earnestly and sternly: *"There is no daylight between us."*

It is invoked often in defense of the US-UK relationship (along with US-Israel, US–Republic of Korea, etc.) and its goal is to eliminate any notion of disagreement. It's catchy. And it's almost always wrong. It denies what we all know: there is daylight between us—between us in any way you define "us"—and denying the gulf doesn't help bridge it. And what a ludicrous standard of agreement to set. Why are we so afraid of daylight?

In our fast-changing and confusing time, this binary idea that we are either the same or we are enemies seems to provide a feeling of temporary security. But the opiate has a terrible side effect. It is dumbing down all of our alliances, both foreign and domestic. On both sides of the Atlantic and on both sides of the political aisle, we are talking at each other, talking past each other, or worse still, not talking to each other at all.

Instead we want to "win." Exactly what, we're not always sure.

My morning of listening to the earnest, wandering, fearful, mirthful thoughts of young Scots on both sides of their independence debate had somehow made me a full convert. Giving a tour d'horizon felt like participating in a Pyramid mindset fantasy. I couldn't pretend anymore, and the joy that swelled up within me was because I knew there was no going back.

# OUT OF THE ARENA

A lot of things we hold dear look different after making the leap to the Constellation mindset. It sheds new light on some things you might not expect, and fair warning: its new light can cast strange shadows and expose flaws in some of our most sacred cows.

My parents got divorced when I was eleven, and that spring my uncle John took me on a long car trip from Boston to South Carolina. Somewhere along the New Jersey Turnpike, I think, he presented me with a challenge that he thought would help make the time pass, provide some needed inspiration, and maybe build a little character too. He asked me to memorize a quotation from Teddy Roosevelt, one of his favorites. By the end of the trip I knew it by heart and it's still up there in my head today. In fact, whenever we gather for big family occasions he usually makes me recite it. He did it at my college graduation and again at my wedding. You've probably heard it.

> It is not the critic who counts; not the man who points out how the strong man stumbles or where the doer of deeds could have done them better. The credit belongs to the man who is actually in the arena, whose face is marred by dust and sweat and blood; who strives valiantly; who errs, who comes short again and again, because there is no effort without error

and shortcoming; but who does actually strive to do the deeds; who knows the great enthusiasms, the great devotions; who spends himself in a worthy cause; who at the best knows in the end the triumph of high achievement, and who at the worst, if he fails, at least fails while daring greatly, so that his place shall never be with those cold and timid souls who neither know victory nor defeat.

My uncle isn't the only fan. Former president Obama quoted it in his eulogy for Republican senator John McCain in a moving ceremony that was a recent rare moment of bipartisanship. Reciting it is a requirement for promotion for US Naval Academy graduates. It inspired Brené Brown's popular TED Talk and the books that followed, including *Daring Greatly*. LeBron James designed a custom Nike basketball shoe with "man in the arena" embossed on the sole.

And I need to confess that now, for me, it inspires frustration.

It's not that I don't get it—I do. It's beautiful and it puts a finger on something very real. To be second-guessed by people who don't have the first clue about whatever it is you are trying your best to do can be anywhere from annoying and frustrating to maddening and infuriating. I've felt this more times than I can count. We all have. And, at the risk of inviting a lot of anger, I don't feel that TR's proposition is very helpful for what I think we all really want: to band together in service of something bigger. I worry that it's a prescription of sorts being liberally handed out by great leaders that encourages (gulp) bad leadership.

I have no quarrel with striving, great enthusiasms, devotions, worthy causes, or failing while daring greatly. On the contrary, all of that is admirable. The frustration for me is more essential than any of that. It's the core image and the essence of the whole perspective: it's gladiatorial—us, alone in the arena, faces "marred by dust and sweat and blood," fighting an unnamed foe, surrounded by others who are critics at worst and neutral onlookers at best. It is highly romantic. But it can be highly toxic.

It presents us with a false choice: fight it out or sit it out. In this mindset, good leadership means winning—winning against your opponent, winning over that crowd, or trying your best to win even if you end up losing. Who's in? Who's out? Who's on top? It's the Pyramid.

When I recited the speech at my wedding I felt I was stepping into something big. Was it into an arena? Who were the critics? Who were we fighting? Of course, our families and friends were all there—were they just bystanders? Co-combatants? Of course not. Nobody won or lost. I knew back then you could lose a marriage (and suspected that fighting it out and sitting it out were the two modes most likely to bring that about), but then and still now I am pretty sure you cannot win one.

Among the American leaders who lived by and passed

along TR's "in the arena" prescription was Richard Nixon, who quoted it in his victory speech in 1968. And quoted it again as the first president to resign from office, six years later. He considered himself a lonely and righteous fighter to the end. There is a catch and cost to this mindset. And we know there's an alternative.

# 7

# A DIFFERENT KIND OF MIGHT

A LONG, UNEASY SILENCE followed on the other end of the telephone call after I gave my answer. The question was simple enough: "What's the title of your talk?" I was back home in America and had been asked to present a keynote speech at a "Best of Leadership Summit," a gathering of people from government, the private sector, and nonprofits to discuss new models of leadership. This was a check-in call with the organizers so they could print the conference materials. Someone on the other end stepped in: "I'm not sure I got it. Could you say it again?" I was fairly sure they had. "Leadership Is a Joke," I repeated. Awkward pauses were more and more common these days.

I reassured them that I didn't think that leadership was a joke in the sense of not being important, but that leadership should be *like* a joke—a good joke—in Jimmy Carr's sense. It remained unclear at the end of the call whether my jokey title met that standard or was itself just a sentence.

After giving the speech, in which I covered some of the ideas that now form this book, I went to a breakout session called "The Key to High-Performing Teams." The presenter was an energetic and informative speaker who began by getting everyone to visualize a day when we were on a team that was truly working well together. Then he asked us to call out our word associations, which included "linked-up," "empowered," and, the most popular one by my informal count, "in flow."

He nodded encouragingly (he had done this before and had heard all those words before), and then he dimmed the house lights and dramatically clicked to project the first slide of his PowerPoint presentation onto the giant screen behind him.

Ha! I laughed.

But then I noticed something. The presenter wasn't smiling at all. Just the opposite. He was earnestly diving into his take on team effectiveness. And I realized the image wasn't ironic. He chose it to represent the cooperative spirit of a good day at the office—to capture all those words we had just yelled out. As I looked around, nobody else seemed particularly bothered.

For my part, I worried about every human in the image. That man jumping over—look at his trajectory. He isn't going to make it. That woman on the left with the safety helmet—it's not her head I am worried about but her hand. Her white jacket is going to be soaked in blood if that leaning-back guy succeeds at inserting his giant gear. And, by the way, who is the guy in the foreground with his back to the camera in the center of the shot—the one doing nothing, looking on with his hands in his pockets? My guess: team leader. Our presenter saw a perfect illustration of a high-functioning team. I saw a meat grinder. Am I overly morbid and sensitive to this stuff? Apparently.

Indeed, this can be one of the occupational hazards of thinking in Constellations. It's hard to unsee the inhumanity of Pyramid thinking at its worst. Sure enough, when I arrived at the Leadership Luncheon, the host organization's new logo was projected on the big screen.

Here it is:

At lunch, I was seated next to a CEO of a Fortune 100 company. The company had recently announced that 1,300 workers would be laid off. I learned too that the company had just posted 1,300 open jobs and was actively recruiting. I asked him the obvious question, which he was also obviously used to answering.

"No," he said flatly. "It's not possible to retrain those thirteen hundred—it's like the difference between nurses and accountants."

I then asked what those eliminated jobs had in common and what, if anything, the new jobs had in common. The first answer came quickly to him, but he delivered it slowly and somberly. He looked down. "Look, if you have the kind of job where you can predict with pretty good precision what your workweek and workflow will look like for the week ahead . . . and the week after that . . . well, then your job is . . ." He paused as if searching for a euphemism and then appeared to give up. "Gone. Or will be gone soon."

The second answer took longer, and his body language changed—he looked back up. "The new jobs are . . . first of all, very different from one another . . . but I guess what they have in common is that we need people who can ask questions of people they barely know . . . questions that no one involved knows the answer to, and together follow those questions wherever they might lead."

So, to sum up: If you can imagine a job in which uncertainty can be eliminated, that's a job that will probably be eliminated. The people who will be hired? Those who can fruitfully embrace uncertainty, following and connecting the branches wherever they might lead.

The struggle sounded familiar. I had heard other executives say they were looking for similar types of people—and having trouble finding them. It's hard to find people with what Follett called the ability to co-create. It's hard to find people with the right mindset to enter into a situation with no predetermined outcome and take a leap with the group and see what might happen—people with what we might call "a different kind of might." And finding them is going to be awfully hard if we keep working under the banner of pyramids and gears.

At nearly all the sixth form colleges in Britain, I was asked by the students about their counterparts in America. How did American students feel about guns and racism and police? I had to admit I had no idea because I was in the UK and, other than my own three kids, I hadn't talked to very many American teenagers. That's why, even though I had no official position or professional reason to continue the high school senior workshops, I kept it up here at home—asking the next generation what they think and feel and what frustrates and inspires them.

The format is the same, but because these are Americans talking about America, not foreigners, the answers are different. And enlightening. From the one-word index cards, the most common answer for what inspires them is "diversity," followed closely by "freedom." What frustrates and concerns them? The most common response is "division"—economic, political, and racial—followed by "loneliness."

Think about that. The thing that inspires them most is diversity and the thing that frustrates them is division. What jumps out is that those words share the same root: *div*, which means separate. So, what they love best and fear most are both rooted in separateness. It feels to them like they have a forced choice—they can fit in only by conforming to a preset mold, and if they reject that in favor of standing out as their true selves, then that means they get left out. Fit in or stand out: pick one.

Let's look at it differently—the opposite of diversity is uniformity and the opposite of division is unity. The students want unity without uniformity. To put it simply: they want to stand out *and* fit in. The Constellation is what younger America is asking for every day, but that's not where we're pointing them.

## PYRAMID PROPAGANDA

The most celebrated and shared advice to young Americans comes at graduation time on our college campuses. This is when we focus on the big picture together as a culture. Good commencement addresses become YouTube classics that we watch over and over. And because grown-ups outnumber students at a typical graduation (if you add up parents, grandparents, and faculty), what we say at graduations tells us a lot about what we all value.

NPR compiled a trove of more than 350 commencement speeches and combed through them to determine the most common messages. Here are the top five:

1. Change the world
2. Listen to your inner voice
3. Work hard
4. Don't give up
5. Embrace failure

Okay, no big surprises. We've heard these many times. They're encouraging us to join the fray. They want us to have the right frame of mind for what's ahead. And at first glance, they appear worthy indeed, especially when we consider the obvious opposite messages:

1. Sit out
2. Shut up
3. Slack off
4. Give up
5. Freak out

Except there is something notable that starts to emerge when you look at them for a while, listed all together. Here they are again:

1. Change the world
2. Listen to your inner voice
3. Work hard
4. Don't give up
5. Embrace failure

Think about it: If you had to draw a picture of someone heeding this advice, what might it look like? For starters, how many people would be in that picture? Just one person all alone, right? It's almost as though we're talking to an astronaut preparing to set off on a solo mission into deep space with no radio contact. "Hey, at least you'll have your inner voice. And, by the way, please return with something that will change the world and save us all. Don't give up!" The advice has all the makings of a great movie, but it is almost nothing like real life.

It's especially incongruous if you compare that image of the lone astronaut with the image of graduation day itself. If you were to stand at that lectern and give the commencement address, you would gaze out and see that these young people are living examples of the fruits of interdependence. Their parents, grandparents, siblings, roommates, and teachers pack the lawn from end to end.

These "others" are usually name-checked by the graduation speaker and applauded. But then a strange thing happens. We get transported to the viewing area at Cape Canaveral, waiting for the students to take off into "real life" on their own, to change the world or die trying.

We pass along the same misleading notion about how ideas and innovation work too. When asked to draw an image for "idea," nearly everyone sketches the exact same thing. And if you do a Google Images search, thousands of versions of that same picture pop up: a yellow incandescent lightbulb strangely floating alone in space—disconnected from anything and everything yet aglow, with little lines emanating from it. Try typing "idea" in a text to a friend, and your smartphone will offer the lightbulb emoji as an alternative. It's a visual cliché we all carry around that is representative of our instinct to isolate, to factor out our interdependence, to think we can do things all by ourselves. An idea is at best an unlit lightbulb. And so are we without other people. To produce our light, we need the same two things a lightbulb needs: energy and a connection.

Of course, the reality is that our students will not enter the solitary airlock chamber of a rocket when they take off the black robes and tasseled caps after graduation. They will find themselves around a table that night probably thinking (and maybe drinking) with some uncertainty about the future. They will find themselves around tables with other people for the rest of their lives. They'll want to make things together. They'll want us all to end the false choice between dependence and independence.

If we want our next generation to develop and strengthen the habits of interdependence, then we need to give that advice, and not subtly (or overtly) pass on Pyramid propaganda.

So how might the Constellation recast the advice from commencement speeches? Let's give it a try.

1. ~~Change the world~~ Change your mindset
2. ~~Listen to your inner voice~~ Share your inner voice
3. ~~Work hard~~ Work through hard things together
4. ~~Don't give up~~ Give up power (to make more)
5. ~~Embrace failure~~ Embrace uncertainty

The Fortune 100 CEO wants employees who can ask difficult questions of people they don't know well. Kids want to be themselves and fit in at the same time. We want flow with teams. Yet we are preaching solitary accomplishment and then sending our young people into organizations that can feel something like meat grinders.

It takes a special kind of strength to take a leap.

Launching into space or running a race (sprint and marathon alike) or fighting it out in the arena are all easier than the truly hard thing: to face yourself and expose your imperfections to others and seek to make something new with them and through them.

Fighting is the easy way out. And remember, there is a cheat sheet on the back of the dollar bill to guide us.

# MIGHT

Several years ago in Charleston, South Carolina, former president Obama gave the eulogy for Reverend Clementa C. Pinckney, a pastor who, along with eight of his congregation, was murdered in his church by a white supremacist. Maybe you even remember that the speech went viral because the president sang "Amazing Grace." But what's interesting is that the song hadn't been written in his speech. It wasn't planned or rehearsed. But he sang anyway and many people in America and around the world were deeply moved. A few days later, the story behind it came out.

The president was flying into Charleston on a helicopter, sitting between his wife, Michelle, and his top adviser, Valerie Jarrett, when he looked up from studying his speech and said, apropos of nothing, "I might sing." They looked at him, confused. What? "I might sing during my speech," he repeated. They both gave him the same look and the same answer: Don't sing. Please. Whatever you do, don't sing. "Well, I might not sing," the president said, "but I think if I sing, the church will sing with me. We'll see how it feels."

So the president arrived and began his eulogy. He reflected on what the church had done in the wake of the tragedy. And he wondered aloud about what our country might do in response. He mentioned that the victims' families had miraculously forgiven the killer. He talked about grace: that with it, anything is possible.

He said: "Amazing grace . . . amazing grace . . ."

And then he paused, for a really long time. In the video, you can see ministers behind him looking up expectantly. To be precise, it was thirteen seconds—which may not sound like a long time but in a speech it's an eternity. In a book, it might look like this:

(not yet)

(still no)

(bit more)

See?

And then the president just started. He began to sing a few bars of "Amazing Grace" all by himself—maybe a little too loudly into his podium microphone.

Then someone called out, "Sing it, Mr. President," and started to sing along. And just as the president had hoped, more people slowly but surely began to join in until the whole congregation was singing.

He could have done the safe thing and just given a moving

speech—Obama knows he is good at that. His singing was . . . well . . . let's say good but not great. But he met the congregation halfway and they were there for him. It was freedom together that helped heal a sorrowful president, congregation, and nation.

He had the power of the pulpit and the microphone and the position and place, and he gave away that power to the congregation. And in so doing, a bloom loop sprung out of those awkward thirteen seconds. Individuals jumped in, joining their voices with Obama's. The congregants needed Obama, but maybe they were surprised to learn that he had come in expecting to need them too. All were changed. And what started it all was the phrase "I might" back in the helicopter.

*Might*, with its two meanings of strength and uncertainty, is a good word for us. Despite what the Pyramid mindset screams at us, "I might" is all right. In fact, it's more than all right—it's all important. All Constellation leaders—known and unknown, remembered and forgotten—begin with that leap. "I might" leads to "I might too," and soon "we might."

Think you might be ready? Not quite certain? Perfect. Now's the time. . . .

# ACKNOWLEDGMENTS

This is a book about leadership and co-creation, and I have so many people to thank who have inspired me and given me the chance to learn about and participate in the power of giving away power and finding freedom together.

There are two women I have always wished I could thank in person for their brilliant power of insight, and for helping me explain a leap in mindset: Mary Parker Follett and Jane Jacobs. And there are two I can thank, have thanked, and must again: Lynne Olson and Lynne Twist. Ambassador John Gilbert Winant showed what can be accomplished when you don't put yourself atop a pedestal. William James and Dorothy Sayers taught me that we are makers of truth and not merely discoverers of truth. Barack Obama, whose diplomatic advice is in this book, also gave me advice about writing it: "Try to write one true thing a day—it's harder than you think." My grandfather, Jacques Barzun, who lived to nearly 105 and wrote more than forty books, cautioned wisely, "Analysis can be incredibly precise, and not remotely accurate" and "Most things in life are not problems to be solved, but difficulties to be dealt with." And, as a bonus, he gave me permission to end sentences with prepositions, which I like to take advantage of.

This book went through many iterations. James Harding read every one, including the first that was thrown in the trash, which, he reassured me in the kindest way possible, was where it belonged. As it evolved, he reminded me that a magazine article or an op-ed can have many ideas, but a book should only have *one*. As I struggled to articulate that one idea, I benefitted enormously from the feedback of: Owsley Brown III, John Hale, Danna Harman, Bella Pollen, Turney Berry, Lt. Colonel Kyle Hurwitz, Emily Bingham, Ann Coffey, Kiff Gallagher, Jon Hill, Leigh Iglehart, Michael Lea, John Johnson, Susan Short, Myrna Boland, Carol Johnston, Larry Kandall, Stephen Kertis, Keven McAlester, Steven Murphy, Ted Smith, and Kate Weinberg. And I benefited from the example and encouragement of: Josh Berger, Ken Burns, Anne Marie Slaughter, David Lammy, Admiral Jim Stavridis, Börje Ekholm, Jenni Russel, Peter Lattman, Steven Tomlinson, A. A. Gill, Alastair Campbell, Geordie Greig, Mark Carney, Vint Cerf, Danny Meyer, Will Oldham, Jimmy Carr, Ewan Venters, Kevin McKenzie, Drew Faust, Andrew Solomon, Adam Hitchcock, Matt Comyns, Phil Deutch, Bill Kennard, Eleni Tsakopoulos-Kounalakis,

Jeffrey Rosen, Hank Meijer, Mark Skinner, Raj Shah, John Griffin, Ben Breier, Will Geyer, Dave Eggers, Stacey Wade, Tom Fox, Mona Sutphen, Heather Kleisner, Ceci Kurzman, Arjun Waney, Dan Baer, Eliane Fattel, Annie Lennox, Danny Rimer, Garvin Brown, Mitch Besser, Fiona Reynolds, Katie Vanneck-Smith, Chiara Brown, Duro Olowu, Rosalyn Dexter, Emma Sullivan, Evan Ryan, Sebastian Scott, Scott Nathan, Augusta Brown Holland, Gill Holland, Farah Pandith, Fred Kleisner, Patrick Healy, J. Harrison, Sam Parker, Macon Phillips, Mark Tokala, Tony Blinken, Cody Kennan, Ben Rhodes, Justine Picardie, and Dwight Poler. And for modeling a pattern and tone of openness and welcome: Ruthie & Richard Rogers. Alain de Botton generously read an early draft, then asked me how much longer I wanted to work on it. I said three months. He nodded with understanding and said he hoped I would give the material three more years. That's exactly what it took, nearly to the day.

Mariana, Lucy, and Charles, my adored siblings, have lovingly and laughingly offered this sort-of-constructive honesty my whole life. Charles, a gifted writer, passed along his mentor's advice to not get freaked out when you feel that what you're writing is, by turns, blatantly obvious or obviously wrong—that's normal. My father has always cared about using the right language to make a point. My mother-in-law, Christy, and my late father-in-law, Owsley, showed me the language and body language of honest-to-goodness inclusiveness. My mother, who has such an abiding faith in leaps of faith, sees and speaks in images and analogies and would be quick to point out in her many rereadings where my phrases struck her as "green" (alive) or "gray" (dead).

This book is only possible because I have been included in teams that try to build big things together. My cousin, friend, and mentor Shelby Bonnie co-founded CNET and gave me the opportunity to work with and learn from all my colleagues there, especially Robin Wolaner. John Kerry gave me an internship, invited me into his campaign, and gifted us all a living example of American diplomacy at its absolute best. Jordan Kaplan and Michael O'Neil, my dear friend and character in these pages, kept calling even when I never picked up. My partners in bringing Obama to Slugger Field, Carolyn Tandy and Brooke Pardue, helped me learn along with all volunteers for Obama '08 to multiply the magic. David Plouffe, Julianna Smoot, and Penny Pritzker kept me and my fellow NFC members focused on success and not status. In 2012: the NFC, David Simas, Joe Rospars, Teddy Goff, Ben LaBolt, Jen O'Malley Dillon, Stephanie Cutter, Buffy Wicks, Jeremy Bird, Liz Jarvis-Shean, Mitch Stewart, Mark Beatty, Michael Blake, Kevin Karlsgodt, Sam Brown, Meaghan Burdick, Liz Lowery, Joe Paulsen, Eugene Chang, Anita Decker Breckinridge, Alyssa Mastromonaco, and so many others showed how to make friction fruitful. And, through it all, my partnership with Rufus Gifford became a great friendship. Before heading overseas, Pete Rouse, Anita Dunn, Tommy Vietor, Jon Favreau, and Walter

Kantsteiner gave me guidance to be myself and be public all at once. My foreign service colleagues and all the members of Mission UK and Mission Sweden—co-led by DCMs Bill Stewart, Liz Dibble, and Lew Lukens—taught me their craft while putting up with my whiteboard doodles. The twenty thousand sixth formers and the members of YLUK helped me understand America better. Graham Hartley gave a master class in the art of daily diplomacy.

Andrew Wylie took me on and gave me permission to be idiosyncratic. Josh Moss took a break from his day job to nudge me to be more like me. Adrian Zackheim pushed me to articulate the right "idea set." And the expertise of Amanda Lang, Mary Kate Skehan, Sarah Brody, Jen Heuer, Jessica Regione, Nicole Celli, Meighan Cavanaugh, Jane Cavolina, and Anna Dobbin transformed my "pages" into a book. Throughout, Merry Sun artfully knew when and when not to push.

Simon Sinek helped me find my "why" with two questions, sparking an ongoing conversation across oceans and continents that I hope never ends. Simon is the indispensable catalyst for making this book a reality.

Then there's the writing of the book itself, word by word, which is a co-creation with someone whose role in this book is hard to define or overstate. So I turn to what novelist Samuel Butler says is the least misleading thing we have: analogy. Rhoades Alderson, a friend since fourteen and a collaborator since 2008, is like a great music producer—a Rick Rubin or

Nile Rodgers—who makes music on both sides of the glass, bringing out (or educing, as Dee Hock might say) not only the best in me, but the best in us, together.

And last and most: to my beloved Brooke, who is the "BBB" in the dedication. She said yes to a blind date, and teaches me every day to see in new ways. And to our three wonderful children, Jacques, Eleanor, and Charles. "You are the future" is the cliché. The reality is that you are the present. In all senses of that word.

# NOTES

## INTRODUCTION

xv **Around the year 2000:** Rhode Island Historical Society, "2020 Vision: Rhode Island Historical Society Strategic Plan Update," www.rihs.org/2020-vision-rhode-island-historical-society -strategic-plan-update/; "Siemens Announces New Company Structure Under Vision 2020+," RTTNews, August 1, 2018, https://mar kets.businessinsider.com/news/stocks/siemens-announces-new -company-structure-under-vision-2020-1027423831#.

xvi **In 2018, with just two years:** Larry Clark, "Is Your 'Vision 2020' Leadership Development Strategy on the Path to Success?," *Harvard Business Publishing Corporate Learning* (blog), August 21, 2018, www.harvardbusiness.org/is-your-vision-2020-leadership -development-strategy-on-the-path-to-success/.

xvi **leaders know their true objective:** Peter F. Ducker, "The Management of Organizations," in *Great Writers on Organizations*, 3rd omnibus ed., eds. Derek S. Pugh and David J. Hickson (Hampshire, UK: Ashgate, 2007), 162.

xxi **Drucker credits her:** Peter F. Drucker, introduction to *Mary Parker Follett, Prophet of Management: A Celebration of Writings from the 1920s*, ed. Pauline Graham (Washington, DC: Beard Books, 1995), 2.

xxi **I am in this book:** Dee Hock, *One from Many: Visa and the Rise of Chaordic Organization* (San Francisco: Berrett-Koehler, 2005), xvi.

## CHAPTER 1: THE LOST CONSTELLATION

2 **Only two signatures appear:** Lewis R. Harley, *The Life of Charles Thomson: Secretary of the Continental Congress and Translator of the Bible from the Greek* (Philadelphia: George W. Jacobs, 1900).

3 **How did they fare:** The story of the logo is based on Richard S. Patterson and Richardson Dougall, *The Eagle and the Shield: A History of the Great Seal of the United States* (Washington, DC: General Printing Office, 1976), 2.

3 **"Moses standing on":** Patterson and Dougall, *Eagle and the Shield*, 14.

3 **Hengist and Horsa:** Patterson and Dougall, *Eagle and the Shield*, 16.

3 **Inspired by a famous:** Patterson and Dougall, *Eagle and the Shield*, 15.

4 **called a *crest*:** Patterson and Dougall, *Eagle and the Shield*, 19–22.

4 **he suggested a potential motto:** Patterson and Dougall, *Eagle and the Shield*, 19–22.

4 **"lie on the table":** Patterson and Dougall, *Eagle and the Shield*, 27.

4 **The design looked like this:** "Second Great Seal Committee—March 1780," http://greatseal.com/committees/secondcomm/index.html.

5 **He called it a "radiant constellation":** Patterson and Dougall, *Eagle and the Shield*, 39.

6 **His official minutes:** Patterson and Dougall, *Eagle and the Shield*, 38.

6 **It was a thirteen-stepped pyramid:** Patterson and Dougall, *Eagle and the Shield*, 68.

7 **"man who tells the truth":** Patterson and Dougall, *Eagle and the Shield*, 71.

7 **"a cancer we must":** Charles Thomson to Thomas Jefferson, November 2, 1785, National Archives, Founders Online, https://founders.archives.gov/documents/Jefferson/01-09-02-0005.

7 **He laid out:** Patterson and Dougall, *Eagle and the Shield*, 60–68.

8 **Here is Thomson's sketch:** "The Final Design of the Great Seal—June 20, 1782," http://greatseal.com/committees/finaldesign/index.html.

9 **They promptly cut:** This image courtesy of the National Archives, *National Archives Identifier 596742,* prologue.blogs.archives.gov/2015/06/20/the-great-seal-celebrating-233-years-of-a-national-emblem/.

9 **It hasn't changed:** Joint Committee on Printing, *Our Flag* (Washington, DC: US Government Printing Office, 2007), 42, www.govinfo.gov/content/pkg/CDOC-109sdoc18/pdf/CDOC-109sdoc18.pdf.

9 **"would come upon us":** Harley, *Life of Charles Thomson,* 108.

10 **president of the Congress:** David McNeely Stauffer, *Seal of the President of the Continental Congress,* 1885, Wikimedia Commons, https://commons.wikimedia.org/w/index.php?curid=83952986.

10 **chose for that position:** Charles A. L. Totten, *The Seal of History: Our Inheritance in the Great Seal of "Manasseh," the United States of America: Its History and Heraldry; and Its Signification Unto "the Great People" Thus Sealed,* vol. 1 (New Haven, CT: Our Race, 1897).

11 **One biographer called Thomson:** Fred S. Rolater, "Charles Thomson, 'Prime Minister' of the United States," *Pennsylvania Magazine of History and Biography* 101, no. 3 (July 1977): 322–48.

11 **He named them after:** Ian W. Toll, *Six Frigates: The Epic History of the Founding of the U.S. Navy* (New York: W. W. Norton, 2006), 58–60.

12 **"Americans of all ages":** Alexis de Tocqueville, *Democracy in America,* ed. and trans. Harvey C. Mansfield and Delba Winthrop (Chicago: University of Chicago Press, 2000), 489.

12 **"I am pained":** Alexis de Tocqueville, in Gary Y. Okihiro et al., *The Great American Mosaic: An Exploration of Diversity in Primary Documents* (Santa Barbara, CA: Greenwood, 2014), 105.

13 **"They easily shake off":** Alexis de Tocqueville, *Democracy in America,* trans. Henry Reeve (Boston: John Allyn, 1876), 547.

14 **He noticed a book:** "How the Pyramid Side of the Great Seal Got on the One-Dollar Bill in 1935," https://greatseal.com/dollar/hawfdr.html.

15 **"to wage a war":** Franklin D. Roosevelt, "Inaugural Address of the President," (speech, Washington, DC, March 4, 1933), National Archives Catalog, https://catalog.archives.gov/id/197333.

**16 Look closely at FDR's:** This image of FDR's notes to the proposed new US dollar bill, engraved by Edward M. Weeks, Bureau of Engraving and Printing, was extracted from a "Commemorating the Seal" poster, part of a State Department exhibition on the Great Seal. See Wikimedia Commons, https://commons.wikimedia.org/wiki/File:1935_Dollar_Bill_Back_Early_Design.jpg.

**16 Final product, issued 1935:** Image obtained from the website of the Littleton Coin Company, dealer in rare money, www.littletoncoin.com.

**21 MIT professor Sherry Turkle:** Sherry Turkle, *Alone Together: Why We Expect More from Technology and Less from Each Other* (New York: Basic Books, 2011).

## CHAPTER 2: CONSTELLATION MAKERS

**25 a temporary classic:** Jeffrey F. Rayport and Thomas A. Gerace, "Encyclopaedia Britannica (A)," Harvard Business School, Case No. 396-051 (1995).

**25 A group of those thinkers:** Shane Greenstein, "The Reference Wars: Encyclopædia Britannica's Decline and Encarta's Emergence," *Strategic Management Journal* 38, no. 5 (May 2017): 995–1017; *Encyclopaedia Britannica Online*, s.v. "Encyclopædia Britannica," by Christopher Hardy Wise Kent et al., updated October 20, 2020, www.britannica.com/topic/Encyclopaedia-Britannica-English-language-reference-work.

**27 It was ostensibly:** Philip Evans and Thomas S. Wurster, *Blown to Bits: How the New Economics of Information Transforms Strategy* (Boston: Harvard Business School Press, 2000), 5.

**31 He called his startup Nupedia:** The story was told to me by Jimmy Wales in London during his visit to the US embassy in 2015. See also Wikipedia, s.v. "History of Wikipedia," last modified October 23, 2020, 14:21, https://en.wikipedia.org/wiki/History_of_Wikipedia; Walter Isaacson, "You Can Look It Up: The Wikipedia Story," *Daily Beast*, July 12, 2017, www.thedailybeast.com/you-can-look-it-up-the-wikipedia-story.

**36 If you don't know:** Dee Hock, *One from Many: Visa and the Rise of Chaordic Organization* (San Francisco: Berrett-Koehler, 2005),

Kindle; see also deehock.com, which has a helpful timeline and history of Visa.

37 **"mechanistic, command-and-control"**: Hock, *One from Many*, 36.

41 **"unimaginably complex and"**: Hock, *One from Many*, 98.

43 **Today, Hock's system**: "Visa Fact Sheet," August 2017, https://usa .visa.com/dam/VCOM/download/corporate/media/visanet -technology/aboutvisafactsheet.pdf.

44 **"to bring or draw forth"**: Hock, *One from Many*, 47.

44 **"our expertise became"**: Dee Hock, "The Birth of the Chaordic Century: Out of Control and Into Order" (speech, Extension National Leadership Conference, Washington, DC, March 11, 1996), www.fs.fed.us/im/philos/chaordic.htm.

45 **"In truth, there"**: Hock, *One from Many*, 172.

## CHAPTER 3: MAKING THE MINDSET

47 **The 2005** *New York Times*: "Obituary: Management Guru Peter F. Drucker Dies," *New York Times*, November 13, 2005, www .nytimes.com/2005/11/13/world/americas/obituary-management -guru-peter-f-drucker-dies.html.

47 **Drucker was number one**: Laurence Prusak and Thomas H. Davenport, "Who Are the Gurus' Gurus?," *Harvard Business Review*, December 2003, https://hbr.org/2003/12/who-are-the-gurus -gurus.

47 **a "social ecologist"**: Peter F. Drucker, *The Daily Drucker: 366 Days of Insight and Motivation for Getting the Right Things Done* (New York: HarperCollins, 2004), 28.

48 **"just about everything"**: Warren Bennis, "Thoughts on 'The Essentials of Leadership,'" in *Mary Parker Follett, Prophet of Management: A Celebration of Writings from the 1920s*, ed. Pauline Graham (Washington, DC: Beard Books, 1995), 178.

48 **"become a 'nonperson'"**: Peter F. Drucker, introduction to *Mary Parker Follett, Prophet of Management: A Celebration of Writings from the 1920s*, ed. Pauline Graham (Washington, DC: Beard Books, 1995), ii.

48 **Mary Parker Follett was born**: I want to thank Joan C. Tonn for her amazing biography of Follett, *Mary P. Follett: Creating*

*Democracy, Transforming Management* (New Haven, CT: Yale University Press, 2003), Kindle.

50 **"all-powerful agency":** Tonn, *Mary P. Follett*, 26.

50 **In essence, the speech:** Tonn, *Mary P. Follett*, 26.

51 **star professor, William James:** "William James," Harvard University, Department of Psychology, https://psychology.fas.harvard .edu/people/william-james.

51 **"Nothing can bring you peace":** Ralph Waldo Emerson, *Essays* (Boston: n.p., 1841), 3.

53 **"'tone,' to be sure,":** William James, "The Social Value of the College-Bred" (address delivered at a meeting of the Association of American Alumnae at Radcliff College, Cambridge, MA, November 7, 1907), www.uky.edu/~eushe2/Pajares/jaCollegeBred.html.

54 **the "unwritten practice":** Mary Parker Follett, *The Speaker of the House of Representatives* (London: Longmans, Green, 1896), xi.

56 **Committee on Substitutes:** Tonn, *Mary P. Follett*, 154.

59 **"Our political life":** Mary Parker Follett, *The New State: Group Organization the Solution of Popular Government* (University Park: Pennsylvania State University Press, 1998), 3.

59 **"that all our work":** "Report of the East Boston Centre by Committee on Extended Use of School Buildings, 1911–1912," *Bulletin: The Women's Municipal League of Boston*, May 1912, 8, quoted in Tonn, *Mary P. Follett*, 210.

61 **"instead of shutting out":** Follett, *New State*, 40.

62 **"the indispensable means":** Follett, *New State*, 292.

63 **Follett had seven terms:** Elliot M. Fox, "Mary Parker Follett: The Enduring Contribution," *Public Administration Review* 28, no. 6 (November–December 1968): 523.

64 *diversity is a fact*: Stephen Frost, *The Inclusion Imperative: How Real Inclusion Creates Better Business and Builds Better Societies* (London: Kogan Page, 2014), 83. Frost was head of diversity and inclusion for the London 2012 Olympic Games. His original phrasing was "Diversity is a reality. Inclusion is a choice."

65 **"at the bottom level":** Tonn, *Mary P. Follett*, 404.

66 **"power-with," not "power-over":** M. P. Follett, *Creative Experience* (London: Longmans, Green, 1924), 189.

67 **her own death:** Tonn, *Mary P. Follett*, 414.

67 *Politics: Who Gets What*: Drucker, introduction to *Mary Parker Follett*, 7.

69 interdependence is ten times: Stephen R. Covey, *The 7 Habits of Highly Effective People* (New York: Free Press, 2004), 324.

71 private and public victory model: This is a sketch of the image that appears in the thirtieth anniversary edition of Covey's *7 Habits of Highly Effective People* (New York: Simon & Schuster, 2020), 213.

73 "never aspired to": Jim Collins, *Good to Great: Why Some Companies Make the Leap and Others Don't* (New York: HarperCollins, 2001), 28, Kindle. See also www.jimcollins.com/concepts/level-five-leadership.html.

73 Yet that's precisely: This is a sketch of the image labeled "Level 5 Hiearchy" that appears in Chapter 3 of Collins's *Good to Great: Why Some Companies Make the Leap and Others Don't* (New York: HarperCollins, 2001).

74 "Cooperation is going": Follett, *New State*, 357.

## CHAPTER 4: LETTING IT GO

75 In Britain's "darkest hour": I relied extensively on Lynne Olson, *Citizens of London: The Americans Who Stood with Britain in Its Darkest, Finest Hour* (New York: Random House, 2010) for this section about Churchill, Winant, and Kennedy.

76 "There's no sense": The stories of Ambassador Kennedy come mostly from David Nasaw, *The Patriarch: The Remarkable Life and Turbulent Times of Joseph P. Kennedy* (New York: Penguin Press, 2012), 498.

77 He was shy: Olson, *Citizens of London*; Bernard Bellush, *He Walked Alone: A Biography of John Gilbert Winant* (The Hague: Mouton, 1968); and Alison R. Holmes and J. Simon Rofe, *The Embassy in Grosvenor Square: American Ambassadors to the United Kingdom, 1938–2008* (London: Palgrave Macmillan, 2012).

77 "There is no place": Olson, *Citizens of London*, 5.

77 "share our purpose": Olson, *Citizens of London*, 25.

78 "in the same boat now": Olson, *Citizens of London*, 144.

79 "Gettysburg at Durham": Bellush, *He Walked Alone*, 186.

80 "This is a wonderful school": Timothy Riley, "The Fulton Report: From the National Churchill Museum," *Finest Hour* 178 (Fall

2017), https://winstonchurchill.org/publications/finest-hour/finest -hour-178/fulton-report-national-churchill-museum/.

81 **Forty-eight stars:** The 1946 US Presidential Seal, as found in Title 3 of the Code of Federal Regulations (CFR), 1943–1948 Compilation, 447.

81 **Truman confided that:** Richard Langworth, "Churchill, Truman and Poker on the Train to Fulton, March 1946," July 6, 2018, https:// richardlangworth.com/churchill-truman-poker-fulton-train.

83 **prescribed a "special relationship":** Winston Churchill, "Sinews of Peace," (speech, Westminster College, Fulton, MO, March 5, 1946), www.nationalchurchillmuseum.org/sinews-of-peace-iron -curtain-speech.html.

84 **"We aim at nothing":** Churchill, "Sinews of Peace."

92 **dubbed "psychological safety":** Charles Duhigg, "What Google Learned from Its Quest to Build the Perfect Team," *New York Times Magazine*, February 25, 2016, www.nytimes.com/2016/02 /28/magazine/what-google-learned-from-its-quest-to-build-the -perfect-team.html. Duhigg quotes Harvard Business School professor Amy Edmondson's definition of the term.

94 **Take an example:** I read an article in a London paper sometime between 2013 and 2017 in which the author called out the difference in habits and behavior between family dinner and family breakfast, and I wish I could remember who it was so I could thank them and credit them for this contrast.

95 **It would require owners:** The stories of the early internet and conversations with the young leaders in the UK are taken from my memory, and from discussions with Vint Cerf before, during, and after the session.

98 ***If you are here to help*:** This is from my memory of how Twist told the story on two different occasions, once during a speech at the Festival of Faiths in Louisville, Kentucky, in April 2017 and again in San Francisco in fall 2018.

98 **"To free the energies":** M. P. Follett, *Creative Experience* (London: Longmans, Green, 1924), 303.

98 **Alcoholics Anonymous was founded:** *Bill W.: A Documentary about the Co-founder of Alcoholics Anonymous*, directed by Dan Carracino and Kevin Hanlon (2012).

100 **"The one valid thing"**: "Alcoholics Anonymous: The Story of How More Than One Hundred Men Have Recovered from Alcoholism," *Journal of the American Medical Association* 113, no. 16 (October 1939): 1513, https://jamanetwork.com/journals/jama/article-abstract/1158635/.

100 **the thirty millionth copy**: Alcoholics Anonymous, "A.A.'s Big Book, Alcoholics Anonymous, Named by Library of Congress as One of the 'Books That Shaped America,'" press release, July 27, 2012, www.aa.org/press-releases/en_US/press-releases/aas-big-book-alcoholics-anonymous-named-by-library-of-congress-as-one-of-the-books-that-shaped-america. And it should be noted that AA didn't send it in an "I told you so" way but rather as a thank-you to the AMA for having categorized alcoholism as a disease many decades before.

101 **It's no secret that:** *Frontline*, season 37, episodes 3–4, "Our Man in Tehran," parts 1 and 2, directed and written by Roel van Broekhoven, featuring Thomas Erdbrink, aired August 13–14, 2018, on PBS. Erdbrink was the Tehran bureau chief for *The New York Times*.

### CHAPTER 5: LETTING IT GROW

103 **Cornfield in Iowa, summer 2007:** Photograph by Charlie Neibergall, Associated Press.

103 **Inauguration Day, winter 2009:** Photograph by Win McNamee, Getty Images.

114 **"I hear you, but no":** This story is from my memory and the quotations are not exact. David Plouffe recounts a much shorter version in his book *The Audacity to Win: The Inside Story and Lessons of Barack Obama's Historic Victory* (New York: Penguin Books, 2009), 49, Kindle.

125 **It's called the snowflake model:** The snowflake model was popularized and promoted by Marshall Ganz, a legendary community organizer and lecturer at Harvard's Kennedy School of Government. See Aaron Wherry, "Q&A: Marshall Ganz on Political Organizing," *Maclean's*, August 27, 2015, www.macleans.ca/politics/qa-marshall-ganz-on-political-organizing/.

128 **above is a sketch:** This is a scan from the British Museum's online copy of Leonardo da Vinci's Notebook reference #83 as found in an article by Marina Mehling, editions.covecollective.org/content /da-vincis-rule-trees.

128 **Like river deltas:** River deltas: Elizabeth Busey. Renaissance at Mossy River. Reduction Linocut as found here: https://elizabeth busey.com/renaissance-makes-its-debu/; Broccoli: Shutterstock photo #1060488929; Neurons: Cerebellum structure. Colored light micrograph of a section through the highly-folded cerebellum of the brain. Licensed from alamy.com.

131 **an "urban activist":** Douglas Martin, "Jane Jacobs, Urban Activist, Is Dead at 89," *New York Times*, April 25, 2006, www .nytimes.com/2006/04/25/books/jane-jacobs-urban-activist -is-dead-at-89.html.

134 **standing up to the bulldozers:** Bill Steigerwald, "City Views," *Reason*, June 2001, https://reason.com/2001/06/01/city-views-2/.

134 **She summed it up:** Sandy Ikeda, "The Great Mind and Vision of Jane Jacobs," Foundation for Economic Education, September 1, 2006, https://fee.org/articles/jane-jacobs/.

134 **"To seek 'causes'":** Jane Jacobs, *The Economy of Cities* (New York: Vintage Books, 1970), 120–21.

## CHAPTER 6: DAYLIGHT BETWEEN US

141 **Here is the poster:** CNET poster, "Friends Don't Let Friends Give Tech Advice," re-creation of the original poster by CNET co-founder Shelby Bonnie.

144 **Obama told the Republicans:** Chuck McCutcheon and David Mark, "'Elections Have Consequences': Does Obama Regret Saying That Now?," *Christian Science Monitor*, November 21, 2014, www.csmonitor.com/USA/Politics/Politics-Voices/2014/1121 /Elections-have-consequences-Does-Obama-regret-saying -that-now.

146 **"All of you are in EUR":** This quotation is a fictionalized example of commentary from a typical State Department Charm School presentation.

169 *The New York Times* ran: Steven Erlanger, "American Ambassador Builds Diplomatic Bridges with British Teenagers," *New York Times*, November 10, 2015, www.nytimes.com/2015/11/11/world/europe/american-ambassador-builds-diplomatic-bridges-with-british-teenagers.html.

177 "It is not the critic": Theodore Roosevelt, "Citizenship in a Republic," (speech, the Sorbonne, Paris, April 23, 1910), www.theodorerooseveltcenter.org/Learn-About-TR/TR-Encyclopedia/Culture-and-Society/Man-in-the-Arena.aspx.

178 My uncle isn't: There are four people referenced in this paragraph about the "in the arena" speech: 1. Obama's eulogy for McCain can be found at Nora Kelly Lee, "Barack Obama's Eulogy for John McCain," *Atlantic*, September 1, 2018, www.theatlantic.com/politics/archive/2018/09/barack-obama-eulogy-john-mccain/569065/; 2. the US Naval Academy requirement can be found on the academy's website, "Common Quandaries," www.usna.edu/TheLOG/faq.php; 3. Brené Brown's use can be found in her TED Talk and Netflix special at https://daretolead.brenebrown.com and https://brenebrown.com; and 4. LeBron James's use of the quote on his sneakers, see Victor Galvez, "LeBron James Wears Kicks with Quote 'Man in the Arena' on Them," Cavs Nation, March 2, 2018, https://cavsnation.com/cavs-news-lebron-james-wears-kicks-with-quote-man-in-the-arena-on-them/.

## CHAPTER 7: A DIFFERENT KIND OF MIGHT

183 the host organization's new logo: The image is a re-creation of the logo done by my friend Shelby Bonnie, based on the original from the conference materials that were not high enough resolution to print in the book.

187 Here are the top five: Jeremy Bowers et al., "The Best Commencement Speeches, Ever," NPR, last updated July 2, 2015, https://apps.npr.org/commencement/.

191 Several years ago in Charleston: Peter Baker, "When the President Decided to Sing 'Amazing Grace,'" *New York Times*, July 6, 2015, www.nytimes.com/politics/first-draft/2015/07/06/obamabaker/.

# SELECTED SOURCES

I want to thank the Wikipedia community contributors, known and unknown, for co-creating such an amazing resource that pointed me to so many of the sources for this book.

Allen, Danielle. *Our Declaration: A Reading of the Declaration of Independence in Defense of Equality.* New York: Liveright Publishing Corporation, 2014.

Barzun, Jacques. *A Stroll with William James.* Chicago: University of Chicago Press, 1984.

Cajete, Gregory. *Native Science: Natural Laws of Interdependence.* Santa Fe: Clear Light Publishers, 2000.

Evans, Philip, and Thomas S. Wurster. *Blown to Bits: How the New Economics of Information Transforms Strategy.* Cambridge, MA: Harvard Business School Press, 2000.

Follett, Mary Parker. *Freedom & Coordination: Lectures in Business Organization,* L.H. Urwick, ed., London: Pitman Publishing, 1949.

Frame, Michael, and Amelia Urry. *Fractal Worlds: Grown, Built, and Imagined.* New Haven: Yale University Press, 2016.

Govindarajan, Vijay, and Praveen Kopalle. "Encyclopedia Britannica (A)." Harvard Business School, Case No. 2-0007 (2001).

Green, Robert. *The 48 Laws of Power.* New York: Penguin Books, 1998.

Hamilton, Schuyler. *History of the National Flag of the United States of America.* Philadelphia: Lippincott, Grambo, 1852.

Hendricks, J. Edwin. *Charles Thomson and the Making of a New Nation, 1729–1824.* Madison, NJ: Fairleigh Dickinson University Press, 1979.

Hunt, Gaillard. *The Seal of the United States: How It Was Developed and Adopted.* Washington, DC: US Department of State, 1892.

Jacobs, Jane. *Vital Little Plans: The Short Works of Jane Jacobs.* Zipp, Samuel, and Nathan Storring, eds. New York: Random House, 2016.

Metcalf, Henry C., and L. Urwick, eds. *Dynamic Administration: The Collected Papers of Mary Parker Follett.* Mansfield Centre, CT: Martino Publishing, 2013.

Moses, Robert. *Public Works: A Dangerous Trade.* New York: McGraw-Hill Inc., 1970.

O'Neil, Paul. "The U.S. Takes Off on Credit Cards." *Life Magazine,* March 1970.

Rayport, Jeffrey F., and Thomas A. Gerace. "Encyclopaedia Britannica (A)." Harvard Business School, Case No. 396-051, 1995. (Revised December 1997.)

Schlenther, Boyd Stanley. *Charles Thomson: A Patriot's Pursuit.* Newark: University of Delaware Press, 1990.

Slaughter, Anne Marie. *The Chess Board and the Web: Strategies of Connection in a Networked World.* New Haven: Yale University Press, 2017.

Smith, James Mitchell. *Undeceived: A Political History of the American Revolution as Inspired by Charles Thomson, Secretary of the*

*Continental Congress, 1774–1789.* Vol. 1. Privately published, CreateSpace, 2016.

Waldrop, M. Mitchell. "The Trillion-Dollar Vision of Dee Hock." *Fast Company,* October 31, 1996.

Winant, John Gilbert. *A Letter from Grosvenor Square: An Account of a Stewardship.* London: Hodder & Stoughton, 1947.